REFLECTIONS: THE ROLE OF POSITIVE MINDSET IN ACHIEVING GOALS

SAJEEV KUMAR K V

To my beloved family, whose unwavering support and love have been my greatest strength.

To the inspiring people of Kerala, whose rich culture and traditions have profoundly shaped my outlook on life.

To the vibrant city of Bangalore, where I found my passion and purpose in the dynamic world of technology.

To all my mentors, colleagues, and friends who have shared this journey with me, providing wisdom, encouragement, and companionship along the way.

And most importantly, to every reader who picks up this book. May you find the courage, inspiration, and positivity to pursue and achieve your dreams.

Contents

Acknowledgements

This book would not have been possible without the support and encouragement of many wonderful people. I would like to take a moment to express my deepest gratitude.

To my parents, for their endless love, guidance, and for instilling in me the values that have shaped who I am today. Your belief in me has been my greatest motivation.

To my family and friends in Kerala, thank you for your unwavering support and for being my constant source of inspiration. Your stories and experiences have greatly influenced my journey.

To my friends and colleagues in Bangalore, the Silicon Valley of India, thank you for the enriching experiences and the countless lessons learned. Your companionship and insights have been invaluable.

To my mentors, who have guided me with their wisdom and experience. Your advice and support have been instrumental in my personal and professional growth.

To the entire team who helped bring this book to life, thank you for your hard work and dedication. Your efforts in editing, designing, and publishing have made this project possible.

To my readers, thank you for your trust and for allowing me to share my journey with you. I hope this book inspires you to cultivate a positive mindset and achieve your goals.

Finally, to everyone who has believed in me and supported me throughout this journey, thank you. This book is a testament to the power of positivity and the incredible impact it can have on our lives.

With heartfelt gratitude,

Sajeev Kumar K. V.

Preface

In the vibrant landscapes of Kerala, amidst the serene backwaters and lush greenery, I discovered the foundational values that have guided my life. Growing up in this beautiful region of India, I learned the importance of community, resilience, and maintaining a positive outlook. These lessons were further enriched by my experiences in Bangalore, the bustling tech hub known as the Silicon Valley of India. It was here that I honed my skills as a tech professional and found my calling as a motivational author.

"Reflections: The Role of Positive Mindset in Achieving Goals" is a culmination of my journey from a curious tech enthusiast to a writer. Throughout this journey, I have encountered numerous challenges and triumphs, each teaching me the invaluable power of maintaining a positive mindset.

This book is not just a collection of theories and principles; it is a reflection of my personal experiences and the stories of those I have met along the way. From the tranquil shores of Kerala to the dynamic streets of Bangalore, I have seen firsthand how a positive mindset can transform lives, drive success, and create lasting impact.

In writing this book, my aim is to share the insights and strategies that have helped me and countless others achieve our goals. Each chapter is designed to provide practical advice, real-world examples, and actionable steps to help you cultivate a positive mindset and unlock your full potential.

Whether you are a student, a professional, or someone simply seeking personal growth, I hope this book serves as a source of inspiration and guidance. The journey towards achieving your goals is often filled with obstacles, but with a positive mindset, you can navigate these challenges and emerge stronger.

Thank you for embarking on this journey with me. I am excited to share these reflections with you and hope they resonate deeply, encouraging you to pursue your dreams with positivity and determination.

With gratitude,

Sajeev Kumar K. V.

Introduction

In a small village in Kerala, surrounded by the tranquility of nature and the warmth of community, my journey began. Growing up in this idyllic setting, I was immersed in a culture that valued resilience, family, and a positive outlook on life. These early experiences laid the groundwork for the mindset that would guide me through the many challenges and opportunities that lay ahead.

As a young tech enthusiast, I was drawn to the vibrant energy of Bangalore, the Silicon Valley of India. The city's dynamic tech scene and entrepreneurial spirit offered endless possibilities, but also demanded perseverance and a relentless drive to succeed. It was here that I truly understood the power of a positive mindset and its critical role in achieving goals.

In my career as a tech professional, I faced numerous obstacles—tight deadlines, complex projects, and the ever-evolving nature of technology. Each challenge tested my resolve and pushed me to find innovative solutions. Through these experiences, I learned that maintaining a positive attitude was not just beneficial, but essential. It enabled me to approach problems with creativity, stay motivated, and inspire my colleagues.

Beyond my professional life, I realized that a positive mindset had a profound impact on my personal growth and relationships. It helped me navigate the ups and downs of life, build meaningful connections, and find joy in everyday moments. This realization fueled my passion for motivational writing, as I wanted to share the transformative power of positivity with others.

"**Reflections:***The Role of Positive Mindset in Achieving Goals*" is a synthesis of my personal experiences, cultural influences, and the lessons I've learned along the way. This book is designed to be a practical guide for anyone looking to cultivate a positive mindset and achieve their goals. Each chapter offers insights, strategies, and real-world examples that can be applied to various aspects of life, from career and relationships to personal development.

As you read through these pages, I encourage you to reflect on your own journey. Embrace the lessons, practice the techniques, and let the stories inspire you. Remember that a positive mindset is a powerful tool that can help you overcome challenges, stay focused on your goals, and lead a fulfilling life.

Thank you for allowing me to share my reflections with you. I hope this book serves as a source of encouragement and empowerment, helping you unlock your full potential and achieve your dreams.

With gratitude,
Sajeev Kumar K. V.

CHAPTER ONE

THE POWER OF POSITIVITY

Growing up in Kerala, I was surrounded by a culture that emphasized the importance of maintaining a positive outlook. Whether it was through the wisdom shared by elders or the vibrant festivals that celebrated life's joys, the message was clear: a positive mindset can transform our experiences and outcomes.

Understanding Positivity and Its Importance

Positivity is more than just a fleeting emotion or a superficial state of mind. It is a profound approach to life that influences our thoughts, actions, and interactions with others. Unlike negativity, which can cloud our judgment and drain our energy, positivity acts as a guiding light, illuminating our path and enabling us to navigate life's challenges with grace and resilience.

Understanding the spectrum between positivity and negativity is crucial. Imagine two individuals facing the same challenging situation at work. The person with a positive outlook sees the challenge as an opportunity to learn and grow, whereas the person with a negative mindset views it as a roadblock, often feeling overwhelmed and defeated. This spectrum highlights where positivity fits in—it is the perspective that transforms potential setbacks into platforms for growth.

The characteristics of positivity are reflected in the behaviours and attitudes of those who embody it. Positive individuals often exhibit optimism, gratitude, and resilience. They approach situations with an open mind, are willing to learn from mistakes, and maintain hope in the face of adversity. This doesn't mean they ignore the realities of life's difficulties;

instead, they choose to focus on solutions and possibilities rather than problems and limitations.

From a cognitive perspective, positivity enhances mental clarity and decision-making. When our minds are not bogged down by negative thoughts, we can think more clearly and make better decisions. Positivity encourages us to see the bigger picture, consider different viewpoints, and weigh our options with a calm and focused mind. This clarity often leads to more effective problem-solving and a greater ability to adapt to changing circumstances.

Historical and Cultural Perspectives

The roots of positivity can be traced back to ancient philosophies and religions that have long recognized its value. In ancient Greek philosophy, the concept of eudemonia, often translated as "human flourishing," was central to the teachings of Aristotle. He believed that true happiness comes from living a virtuous life and achieving one's full potential. This idea aligns closely with modern interpretations of positivity, which emphasize personal growth and fulfilment.

Similarly, in Eastern philosophies, positivity is deeply ingrained. Buddhism, for example, teaches the importance of maintaining a positive outlook through the practice of mindfulness and compassion. The Buddhist concept of "right thinking" encourages individuals to cultivate thoughts that are kind, loving, and free from negativity. This approach fosters a positive mindset that can lead to inner peace and contentment.

Cultural variations also play a significant role in how positivity is viewed and practiced. In collectivist cultures, such as those in many parts of Asia and Africa, positivity is often linked to community well-being and social harmony. In these cultures, maintaining a positive attitude is seen as a way to support the greater good and strengthen social bonds. In contrast, individualistic cultures, such as those in the United States and Western Europe, may emphasize personal achievement and self-improvement as pathways to positivity.

In contemporary society, the concept of positivity has evolved to encompass a wide range of practices and beliefs. The rise of positive psychology as a scientific field has brought attention to the benefits of fostering positive emotions and experiences. This shift has led to an increased focus on well-being, resilience, and the cultivation of positive habits that support a fulfilling life.

Importance of Positivity

The importance of positivity cannot be overstated, particularly when it comes to health. Numerous studies have shown that maintaining a positive mindset can have significant physical and mental health benefits. Positivity has been linked to lower stress levels, reduced risk of chronic diseases, and increased longevity. For instance, research suggests that individuals with a positive outlook are less likely to experience the harmful effects of stress, as they tend to cope with challenges more effectively and recover more quickly from setbacks.

In addition to its impact on health, positivity plays a crucial role in fostering better personal and professional relationships. Positive individuals tend to be more approachable, empathetic, and understanding, which helps them build strong connections with others. In the workplace, positivity can lead to improved collaboration and teamwork, as it encourages open communication and mutual support. In personal relationships, a positive attitude can enhance intimacy and trust, creating a nurturing environment where love and respect can thrive.

The overall well-being of individuals is also significantly influenced by positivity. People who maintain a positive mindset often report higher levels of life satisfaction and happiness. They are more likely to pursue meaningful goals and engage in activities that bring them joy and fulfilment. Positivity helps individuals develop a sense of purpose and direction, which is essential for achieving long-term success and contentment.

A story that illustrates the transformative power of positivity comes from a tech professional who faced a daunting challenge early in his career. After working tirelessly on a project that ultimately failed, he could have easily succumbed to negativity and self-doubt. However, he chose to embrace a positive mindset, viewing the experience as a valuable learning opportunity. By reflecting on what went wrong and identifying areas for improvement, he was able to grow both personally and professionally. This shift in perspective not only helped him overcome the initial setback but also paved the way for future successes.

In conclusion, positivity is a powerful force that can profoundly impact our lives. By understanding its significance and embracing its principles, we can unlock our full potential, build meaningful relationships, and achieve lasting success and happiness. Whether through cultivating a positive mindset, learning from historical and cultural perspectives, or recognizing its importance in our daily lives, positivity offers a pathway to a more fulfilling and rewarding life.

How a Positive Mindset Influences Success?

Success in any endeavour—whether it's achieving career goals, building strong relationships, or fostering personal growth—is significantly influenced by our mindset. A positive mindset, characterized by optimism, resilience, and a proactive attitude, plays a crucial role in shaping our experiences and outcomes. Let's delve into the various ways in which a positive mindset influences success across different areas of life:

The Connection Between Mindset and Outcomes

In the realm of personal and professional success, mindset is a powerful determinant of outcomes. A positive mindset not only shapes how we perceive and react to our environment but also fundamentally alters the way we perform and achieve our goals. The connection between mindset and outcomes is evident in the way positivity enhances productivity and performance. When we approach tasks with a positive attitude, we are more likely to engage fully, remain focused, and persist in the face of difficulties.

A positive mindset acts as a catalyst for resilience and adaptability. In a rapidly changing world, the ability to bounce back from setbacks and adapt to new circumstances is crucial. Positivity provides a buffer against stress and helps individuals navigate challenges with grace. Consider a software developer who encounters a major bug just before a product launch. Instead of succumbing to panic and frustration, a positive mindset allows them to view the bug as a puzzle to be solved. This shift in perspective reduces stress and opens up creative problem-solving avenues, ultimately leading to a successful resolution.

Moreover, a positive mindset fuels motivation and drive. When we focus on our goals through positive reinforcement, we create a cycle of success. Positive affirmations and visualization techniques help maintain a clear vision of our objectives, making it easier to stay motivated even when the going gets tough. For instance, an entrepreneur embarking on a new venture may face numerous challenges, but by maintaining a positive mindset, they can keep their eyes on the prize and remain driven to overcome obstacles.

Positivity and Leadership

The influence of a positive mindset is particularly pronounced in leadership. Inspirational leaders understand that their mindset directly impacts their team's morale and performance. A leader who approaches challenges with optimism and confidence can inspire their team to do the same. By demonstrating resilience and a solution-oriented attitude, positive leaders create an environment where team members feel empowered to take initiative and contribute their best efforts.

Building trust is another essential aspect of positive leadership. When leaders consistently interact with their team in a positive and supportive manner, they establish credibility and foster trust. Trust is the foundation of any successful team, and it is built through transparent communication, empathy, and encouragement. Consider a manager who regularly acknowledges their team's achievements and provides constructive feedback. This approach not only boosts morale but also strengthens the team's commitment to shared goals.

Positivity also plays a vital role in encouraging innovation. In a positive work environment, individuals are more likely to feel safe taking risks and exploring new ideas. A positive leader nurtures creativity by fostering a culture of openness and curiosity. For example, in a tech company, a leader who celebrates experimentation and rewards innovative thinking is more likely to inspire breakthroughs and drive the organization forward.

Overcoming Obstacles

Life is full of obstacles, but a positive mindset can transform these challenges into opportunities for growth. One effective technique for overcoming obstacles is positive reframing. By consciously choosing to view challenges from a different perspective, we can change our response to them. For instance, when faced with a demanding project deadline, rather than viewing it as a source of stress, we can see it as a chance to develop time management skills and enhance our ability to work under pressure.

Problem-solving is another area where positivity proves invaluable. A solution-oriented mindset enables us to approach problems with creativity and confidence. Instead of dwelling on what went wrong, positive thinkers focus on identifying solutions and implementing them effectively. This proactive approach not only leads to better outcomes but also builds resilience, as individuals become adept at handling setbacks and learning from mistakes.

Sustaining momentum through long-term challenges requires a commitment to maintaining positivity. It's important to acknowledge that setbacks are a natural part of any journey and that persistence is key to overcoming them. A positive mindset helps individuals stay focused on their goals, even when progress is slow or obstacles seem insurmountable. By celebrating small victories along the way and staying committed to their vision, individuals can maintain the motivation needed to achieve long-term success.

Practical Advice and Personal Stories

To illustrate the power of a positive mindset in action, let's consider the story of a young professional navigating their career in the tech industry. Early in their career, they faced a series of challenges, including tight deadlines, complex projects, and unexpected setbacks. However, by cultivating a positive mindset, they were able to approach each challenge with determination and creativity.

For example, when tasked with leading a cross-functional team to develop a new software feature, the professional encountered resistance from team members who were skeptical of the project's feasibility. Instead of succumbing to negativity, they chose to lead by example, demonstrating optimism and a belief in the team's capabilities. By fostering open communication and encouraging collaboration, they were able to build trust and inspire the team to work together toward a common goal. The project not only succeeded but also strengthened the team's bond and set the stage for future achievements.

Another story highlights the role of positivity in overcoming personal obstacles. During a challenging period marked by setbacks and uncertainty, the individual found solace in positive reframing. By shifting their focus from what was going wrong to what they could learn from the experience, they were able to maintain resilience and adaptability. This mindset shift allowed them to identify new opportunities for growth and development, ultimately leading to a breakthrough in their career.

In conclusion, a positive mindset is a powerful tool that can significantly influence success in both personal and professional endeavours. By understanding the connection between mindset and outcomes, embracing positivity in leadership, and leveraging positivity to overcome obstacles, individuals can unlock their full potential and achieve lasting success. The stories and practical advice shared in this chapter highlight the transformative power of positivity and serve as a reminder that success is within reach when approached with a positive mindset. As we continue to explore the impact of positivity in the chapters ahead, it becomes clear that cultivating a positive mindset is not just a choice; it is a pathway to a more fulfilling and rewarding life.

Real-Life Tech Career Examples

Throughout my techie life, I have encountered numerous challenges and successes that underscore the transformative power of a positive mindset. Here are some real-life examples that illustrate how positivity has influenced my career:

Early Career Challenges

My techie life began with the role of a technical support executive. As a fresh graduate with limited experience, I was enthusiastic yet anxious about what lay ahead. The reality of the tech world soon hit me hard, as I faced the pressure of solving complex issues while managing customer expectations. This initial phase was a baptism by fire, teaching me valuable lessons in resilience and the power of positivity.

One of my first challenges was dealing with a major network outage that left clients frustrated and our team scrambling for solutions. As a technical support person, I was on the frontline, handling calls from irate customers while trying to diagnose the issue. The stress was palpable, and it would have been easy to succumb to negativity. However, I realized that maintaining a positive attitude was crucial, not only for my own sanity but also for the morale of the entire team.

Instead of viewing the situation as an insurmountable obstacle, I saw it as an opportunity to learn and grow. I collaborated closely with my colleagues, leveraging each person's strengths to tackle the problem methodically. This experience taught me the importance of staying calm under pressure and viewing setbacks as stepping stones. By maintaining a positive outlook, we were able to resolve the issue, and I emerged from the experience with newfound confidence in my abilities.

Leading Projects with Positivity

As I progressed in my career to roles like network technician and system/ network administrator, I began to take on leadership responsibilities. One of the most rewarding aspects of this journey was discovering the transformative power of positivity in fostering collaboration and teamwork.

In one notable project, I was tasked with leading a team to implement a new IT infrastructure for a large organization. The project was ambitious, involving multiple stakeholders and tight deadlines. From the outset, I knew that a positive approach would be essential in guiding the team through the challenges ahead.

I made it a priority to create an environment where every team member felt valued and empowered to contribute their ideas. By fostering open communication and encouraging a collaborative spirit, we were able to harness the diverse skills and perspectives within the team. This positivity not only enhanced our problem-solving capabilities but also strengthened our bonds, creating a sense of camaraderie that fuelled our success.

In parallel, maintaining a positive relationship with our clients was crucial. During client meetings, I focused on understanding their needs and addressing their concerns with empathy and transparency. By approaching client relations with positivity, we built trust and rapport, paving the way for a successful partnership. The project was delivered on time, exceeding client expectations and reinforcing the impact of positivity in building strong client partnerships.

Innovation and Growth

Throughout my career, the power of positivity has been a driving force behind innovation and personal growth. As I moved into roles such as NOC team leader and IT infrastructure manager, I embraced the challenges and opportunities that came with these positions, using positivity as a catalyst for creativity and advancement.

One memorable instance involved a project where we needed to overhaul our network infrastructure to accommodate rapid growth. The task was daunting, requiring out-of-the-box thinking and innovative solutions. Rather than being overwhelmed by the complexity of the project, I encouraged my team to approach it with enthusiasm and a can-do attitude.

By fostering a positive mindset, we were able to brainstorm and develop creative solutions that not only addressed the immediate challenges but also positioned the company for future growth. This experience highlighted the role of positivity in driving innovation, as it empowers individuals to explore new ideas and take calculated risks.

On a personal level, embracing positivity has been instrumental in my professional development. It has taught me the value of continuous learning and adaptability, enabling me to stay abreast of technological advancements and industry trends. By focusing on the possibilities rather than limitations, I have been able to seize opportunities that align with my career aspirations, contributing to my growth as an IT professional.

Mentorship Experience

One of the most fulfilling aspects of my career has been the opportunity to mentor junior colleagues and aspiring tech professionals. As I moved into leadership positions such as IT Head, I recognized the importance of nurturing the next generation of talent and fostering a culture of positivity within the industry.

Mentorship is a powerful tool for both personal and professional growth. It allows experienced individuals to share their knowledge and experiences, while mentees gain valuable insights and guidance. I have always approached mentorship with a positive mindset, focusing on empowering others to achieve their full potential.

One memorable mentorship experience involved a young technician who was struggling to find his footing in the tech world. He was talented but lacked confidence and direction. Drawing from my own experiences, I offered guidance and support, emphasizing the importance of maintaining a positive mindset and viewing challenges as opportunities for growth. Through regular one-on-one sessions, I encouraged him to embrace a positive mindset and view challenges as opportunities for growth. Together, we set achievable goals and worked on building his skills and confidence.

Over time, I witnessed a remarkable transformation in his attitude and performance. He began to tackle challenges with enthusiasm and developed a proactive approach to problem-solving. This experience reinforced the power of positivity in mentorship, as it not only benefits the mentee but also enriches the mentor's perspective and reinforces the importance of a supportive and positive work environment.

Reflections and Takeaways

Reflecting on my techie life, it is clear that positivity has been a guiding light in navigating the complexities and challenges of this dynamic field. The lessons learned from applying positivity to real-life situations have provided a foundation for success and fulfilment.

One key takeaway is the importance of maintaining a growth mindset, where challenges are viewed as opportunities for learning and improvement. This perspective not only enhances resilience but also cultivates a proactive approach to overcoming obstacles. By focusing on possibilities rather than limitations, I have been able to seize opportunities that align with my aspirations and contribute meaningfully to the tech industry.

Looking ahead, positivity continues to influence my career goals and aspirations. As I navigate new challenges and opportunities, I carry with me the knowledge that a positive mindset is not just a tool for success but a way of life that enriches both personal and professional experiences.

In conclusion, the power of positivity has been a defining factor in my techie life. From navigating early challenges to leading projects and driving innovation, positivity has been a constant companion, guiding me toward success and fulfillment. Through personal stories and practical advice, it is evident that a positive mindset is not only a catalyst for achieving goals but also a source of resilience, creativity, and growth.

Conclusion

The power of positivity lies in its ability to transform our perspective and approach to life. By cultivating a positive mindset, we can enhance our health, relationships, career, and personal growth. It equips us to face challenges with resilience, stay motivated, and inspire those around us.

In the following chapters, we will delve deeper into the practical aspects of maintaining a positive mindset and explore how it can be applied to various facets of life. As you embark on this journey, I encourage you to reflect on your own experiences and consider how positivity has played a role in your life. Embrace the power of positivity, and let it guide you towards achieving your goals and realizing your fullest potential.

CHAPTER TWO

THE KERALA PERSPECTIVE

Growing up in the culturally rich and vibrant state of Kerala has deeply influenced my perspective on positivity and success. Known as "God's Own Country," Kerala's lush landscapes, rich traditions, and resilient community spirit have shaped my values and approach to life and career. In this chapter, we explore how the Kerala perspective has imbued me with a unique outlook that enhances my journey towards personal and professional fulfilment.

Cultural Influences of Kerala on Mindset and Attitude

Growing up in Kalliassery, a village in the Kannur district of Kerala, I was immersed in culture rich in community values, educational emphasis, and spiritual depth. These elements have profoundly shaped my mindset and attitude, providing a foundation for resilience, adaptability, and positivity in my personal and professional life.

The Role of Community and Family

In Kerala, community and family play pivotal roles in shaping individuals. In Kalliassery, where I spent my formative years, the bonds within the community were strong and supportive. We lived as an extended family, where neighbours knew each other, shared joys and sorrows, and participated in each other's lives.

The sense of community was palpable during the many cultural programs and sports events I was involved in. Organizing football tournaments and cultural events with club members taught me the power of collaboration and teamwork. We worked together towards common goals, whether it was setting up a stage for a cultural program or preparing the field for a football match. These experiences instilled in me the importance of cooperation and mutual support, which I have carried into my professional life.

Family traditions were equally significant in shaping my outlook. Growing up, my family emphasized values such as respect, kindness, and empathy. We celebrated festivals like Onam, Navratri, Vishu, etc. together, which were not just occasions for joy but also opportunities to reinforce familial bonds. During Onam, we would create intricate flower carpets, a tradition that required patience and teamwork. The Navratri festival at the Bhagavati temple and the fireworks during the Vishu festival were family events that brought us closer, teaching us the importance of togetherness and shared happiness. These experiences fostered a positive mindset, rooted in the belief that we are stronger together.

Education and Literacy

Kerala is renowned for its high literacy rates and emphasis on education, which have been instrumental in shaping the minds and attitudes of its people. My journey in Kalliassery was no exception, as education played a central role in my development.

The importance of education was ingrained in us from an early age. The local schools were not just centres of learning but also community hubs where ideas were exchanged, and critical thinking was encouraged. Education was seen as a tool for personal development and empowerment, allowing us to question, explore, and innovate. This environment nurtured my curiosity and desire to learn, which have been vital in my career, enabling me to adapt to the ever-changing landscape of the tech industry.

The cultural value placed on education in Kerala extends beyond formal schooling. It fosters a mindset of lifelong learning, where acquiring knowledge is a continuous process. This attitude was evident in the community, where discussions about books, science, and current affairs were commonplace. I remember lively debates with friends and family about the latest developments in technology and how they could be applied to improve our community. This culture of learning and adaptation has been crucial in my professional life, encouraging me to stay updated with the latest technological advancements and apply them innovatively.

Spiritual and Philosophical Outlook

Kerala's diverse spiritual traditions and philosophical teachings have significantly influenced the mindset and attitude of its people, including mine. These elements have provided a framework for developing a balanced and peaceful mindset.

In Kalliassery, spiritual practices were an integral part of life. The local temples were not just places of worship but also centers of community gatherings and cultural events. Participating in festivals like the Navratri festival at the Bhagavati temple offered opportunities for reflection and introspection. These spiritual practices fostered a sense of inner peace and balance, helping me navigate life's challenges with equanimity and grace.

Traditional philosophical teachings in Kerala emphasize values such as compassion, resilience, and the interconnectedness of all life. These teachings have profoundly shaped my perspective, encouraging me to approach challenges with a positive and open mind. For instance, the concept of "*Samatva*", or equanimity, taught me to maintain balance and composure in the face of adversity. This philosophy has been instrumental in my professional life, allowing me to stay calm and focused during challenging situations and approach problems with a solution-oriented mindset.

Personal Reflections

Reflecting on my journey, the cultural influences of Kerala have played a crucial role in shaping my mindset and attitude. The strong community bonds and family values instilled a sense of empathy and collaboration. The emphasis on education and lifelong learning fostered a mindset of curiosity and adaptability. The spiritual and philosophical teachings provided a framework for developing resilience and maintaining a positive outlook.

These cultural influences have been invaluable in my personal and professional life. They have taught me to view challenges as opportunities for growth, approach problems with an open mind, and foster positive relationships with those around me. As I continue my journey, I carry these lessons with me, guided by the wisdom of Kerala's rich cultural heritage.

In conclusion, the cultural influences of Kerala have profoundly shaped my mindset and attitude, providing a foundation for success and happiness. The role of community and family, the emphasis on education, and the spiritual and philosophical outlook have instilled in me values of empathy, resilience, and positivity. These lessons have been instrumental in my personal and professional journey, guiding me toward a fulfilling and purposeful life.

Lessons from Kerala's Rich Heritage and Traditions

Growing up in Kalliassery, a village in the Kannur district of Kerala (often referred to as "God's Own Country,"), I was deeply influenced by the rich heritage and traditions of the region. These experiences have imparted valuable lessons that have shaped my mindset and approach to life. Kerala's vibrant arts, sustainable living practices, and historical resilience offer profound insights into creativity, community, and adaptability.

Traditional Arts and Culture

The traditional arts and culture of Kerala are not just forms of entertainment but powerful expressions of creativity and community bonding. Participating in cultural programs and organizing events with friends and family allowed me to witness firsthand the transformative impact of these art forms.

Kerala is renowned for its rich tradition of performing arts, including Kathakali, Theyyam, and Mohiniyattam. These art forms are not merely performances but intricate storytelling mediums that convey deep philosophical and moral lessons. Growing up, I was captivated by the vibrant costumes, elaborate makeup, and expressive movements of Kathakali artists who performed in the local temple during festivals. The performances, often based on stories from Indian epics, taught me the power of creativity and expression. They inspired me to appreciate the beauty of storytelling and the ability to convey complex emotions and ideas through art.

Theyyam, another traditional art form, holds a special place in the cultural fabric of Kerala. It is a ritualistic performance that embodies the spiritual connection between the performer and the divine. Attending Theyyam performances in my village was a transformative experience, as it instilled a sense of reverence for tradition and spirituality. These art forms have taught me the importance of embracing creativity and expression in my personal and professional life, encouraging me to think outside the box and approach challenges with a creative mindset.

Festivals in Kerala, such as Onam, Vishu, Navratri, etc. are vibrant celebrations that promote community bonding and positivity. Growing up, these festivals were significant events in our village, bringing people together in joyous celebration. Onam, the harvest festival, was marked by the creation of intricate flower carpets, known as *pookalam,* which required teamwork, patience, and attention to detail. Participating in these competitions taught me the value of collaboration and the joy of creating something beautiful together.

Vishu, the Malayali New Year, was celebrated with fireworks and feasts, symbolizing new beginnings and prosperity. The festival's emphasis on hope and renewal resonated with me, instilling a positive outlook on life and the belief in fresh starts and endless possibilities. Navratri, celebrated with vibrant cultural programs and traditional dances, reinforced the importance of community engagement and cultural preservation. These festivals have imparted valuable lessons on the power of community, positivity, and shared experiences in fostering a sense of belonging and happiness.

Sustainable Living Practices

Kerala's heritage is deeply rooted in sustainable living practices, reflecting a profound respect for nature and a commitment to holistic well-being. Growing up in Kalliassery, I was surrounded by lush greenery and witnessed the harmony between people and the environment.

Kerala's agricultural practices emphasize sustainable living and a deep connection with nature. The region's traditional farming methods prioritize biodiversity, crop rotation, and organic practices, ensuring environmental balance and sustainability. Growing up, I participated in community farming activities, learning the importance of working in harmony with nature and respecting the land that sustains us. These experiences instilled in me a sense of responsibility towards the environment and the importance of sustainable practices in our daily lives.

This connection with nature extends beyond agriculture to the preservation of natural resources. Kerala's abundant water bodies, including rivers, lakes, and backwaters, are integral to the state's identity and way of life. The community's efforts to preserve these resources taught me the importance of environmental stewardship and the need to protect and cherish our natural heritage for future generations.

Ayurveda and Wellness

Kerala's rich tradition of Ayurveda, a holistic system of medicine, emphasizes the integration of mind, body, and spirit for overall well-being. Growing up, I witnessed the widespread use of Ayurvedic practices in my community, from herbal remedies to therapeutic treatments. Ayurveda taught me the importance of a balanced lifestyle and the need to prioritize self-care and wellness.

The emphasis on natural remedies and preventive care resonated with me, encouraging me to adopt a holistic approach to health and well-being. Ayurveda's focus on balance and harmony aligns with the principles of mindfulness and self-awareness, which have been instrumental in maintaining a positive mindset and resilience in my personal and professional life.

Historical Resilience

Kerala's history is marked by resilience and adaptability, shaped by its experiences of colonization, trade, and cultural exchange. These historical influences have instilled a mindset of perseverance and innovation in the people of Kerala.

Kerala's colonial history, marked by foreign rule and resistance, has shaped a resilient and adaptive mindset among its people. Growing up, I learned about the struggles and triumphs of Kerala's freedom fighters and their unwavering determination to reclaim their land and identity. These stories of resilience and courage taught me the importance of standing up for one's beliefs and the power of collective action in overcoming adversity.

The historical challenges faced by Kerala have instilled a sense of tenacity and adaptability, encouraging me to approach challenges with a positive and solution-oriented mindset. This resilience has been instrumental in navigating the complexities of the tech industry, allowing me to adapt to changing circumstances and embrace new opportunities.

Kerala's history as a hub of trade and cultural exchange has fostered a spirit of diversity and innovation. The region's strategic location along ancient trade routes facilitated the exchange of goods, ideas, and cultures, enriching Kerala's heritage and identity. Growing up, I was exposed to diverse cultural influences, from art and cuisine to language and customs. This exposure instilled in me an appreciation for diversity and the importance of embracing new ideas and perspectives.

The lessons from Kerala's history of trade and exchange have encouraged me to adopt an open and inclusive mindset, fostering creativity and innovation in my personal and professional endeavors. The ability to embrace diversity and adapt to change has been a valuable asset in the tech industry, allowing me to collaborate with diverse teams and explore innovative solutions to complex problems.

Personal Reflections

Reflecting on my journey, the lessons from Kerala's rich heritage and traditions have profoundly shaped my mindset and approach to life. The traditional arts and culture have taught me the importance of creativity and community bonding. The sustainable living practices have instilled in me a sense of responsibility towards the environment and holistic well-being. The historical resilience of Kerala has encouraged me to embrace diversity and innovation while maintaining a resilient and adaptive mindset.

These lessons have been invaluable in my personal and professional journey, guiding me toward a fulfilling and purposeful life. They have taught me to approach challenges with a positive and open mind, foster meaningful connections with others, and embrace creativity and innovation in all aspects of life.

In conclusion, the rich heritage and traditions of Kerala offer profound insights into creativity, community, and adaptability. The lessons from Kerala's traditional arts and culture, sustainable living practices, and historical resilience have shaped my mindset and approach to life, guiding me toward a positive and purposeful journey. These lessons continue to inspire me to embrace positivity and resilience in all aspects of my life, empowering me to overcome challenges and achieve success.

Shaping My Outlook on Life and Work

Growing up in Kalliassery, a village in the Kannur district of Kerala, my life has been deeply influenced by the rich cultural heritage and traditions of my homeland. The lessons I learned from this vibrant culture have shaped my personal values, professional growth, and vision for the future. From the strong community ties to the emphasis on integrity and innovation, these influences have guided me in navigating life's challenges and pursuing my goals with purpose and passion.

Personal Values and Ethics

The values instilled in me during my formative years in Kerala have profoundly influenced my approach to life and work. These values form the foundation of my ethical decision-making and interpersonal relationships.

Integrity and Honesty

In Kerala, integrity and honesty are deeply ingrained cultural values. Growing up, I was taught the importance of standing by one's principles and being truthful in all interactions. My family and community emphasized the significance of honesty, not just as a moral obligation but as a way of building trust and credibility with others.

This commitment to integrity has been a guiding principle throughout my career. Whether making tough decisions or navigating complex challenges, I have always prioritized honesty and transparency. For instance, during a challenging project in my role as a team leader in the tech industry, I faced a situation where meeting a deadline seemed impossible without compromising on quality. Instead of taking shortcuts, I chose to be transparent with the client about the challenges we were facing and proposed a revised timeline that ensured the project's success without sacrificing quality. This decision not only preserved our relationship with the client but also reinforced the team's commitment to ethical standards.

Empathy and Compassion

Kerala's community-oriented values have instilled in me a deep sense of empathy and compassion for others. Growing up, I witnessed how my community came together to support one another during festivals, celebrations, and even challenging times. This sense of belonging and collective support taught me the importance of understanding and caring for others.

In my professional life, empathy and compassion have played a crucial role in building strong interpersonal relationships. As a leader, I have strived to create an inclusive and supportive work environment where team members feel valued and understood. One of the most rewarding experiences in my career was mentoring a junior colleague who was struggling with adapting to a new role. By taking the time to listen to their concerns and providing guidance, I was able to help them overcome their challenges and grow in confidence and capability. This experience reinforced the power of empathy and compassion in fostering positive relationships and driving collective success.

Professional Growth and Development

The lessons from Kerala have been instrumental in shaping my professional growth and development. The region's emphasis on resilience, collaboration, and innovation has guided my approach to navigating challenges and building successful teams.

Adaptability and Innovation

Kerala's history of resilience in the face of challenges has taught me the importance of adaptability and innovation. Growing up in a community that thrived on resourcefulness and creativity, I learned to view challenges as opportunities for growth and innovation.

In my techie life, I have applied these lessons to navigate professional challenges and drive innovation. One memorable experience was leading a project to develop a new software solution for a client with specific requirements. The project faced numerous obstacles, from technical complexities to changing client expectations. However, by fostering a culture of adaptability and encouraging innovative thinking within the team, we were able to overcome these challenges and deliver a solution that exceeded the client's expectations. This experience highlighted the value of resilience and innovation in achieving success in dynamic and competitive environments.

Collaboration and Teamwork

The cultural influences of Kerala have also shaped my approach to collaboration and teamwork. Growing up, I actively participated in sports such as football, cricket, and badminton, where teamwork and camaraderie were essential for success. Organizing football tournaments and cultural events with club members further reinforced the importance of working together towards a common goal.

In my professional life, I have carried these lessons into my approach to building positive work environments. As a leader, I prioritize fostering a culture of collaboration and inclusivity, where team members are encouraged to share ideas and work together towards shared objectives. One of the most fulfilling aspects of my career has been witnessing the power of teamwork in driving innovation and achieving outstanding results. By creating an environment that values diverse perspectives and encourages open communication, I have been able to harness the collective strengths of the team to tackle complex challenges and deliver exceptional outcomes.

Vision for the Future

The lessons from Kerala's rich heritage and traditions have not only shaped my personal and professional growth but have also inspired my vision for the future. Balancing tradition and modernity and contributing to society are integral to this vision.

Balancing Tradition and Modernity

Growing up in Kerala, I learned the importance of balancing tradition and modernity in pursuing personal and professional goals. The region's cultural heritage and emphasis on preserving traditional values while embracing progress have influenced my approach to integrating traditional wisdom with modern advancements.

In my personal life, I strive to incorporate traditional practices, such as mindfulness and holistic wellness, into my daily routine to maintain balance and well-being. Professionally, I am committed to leveraging the latest technologies and innovations to drive progress while staying rooted in ethical and sustainable practices. By embracing both tradition and modernity, I believe it is possible to achieve a harmonious and fulfilling life that aligns with one's values and aspirations.

Contributing to Society

The lessons from Kerala have also inspired a strong commitment to social responsibility and community development. Growing up, I witnessed how my community came together to support one another during festivals, celebrations, and times of need. This sense of collective responsibility has influenced my desire to contribute positively to society.

Throughout my career, I have sought opportunities to give back to the community, whether through volunteering, mentorship, or supporting initiatives that promote education and well-being. One of my aspirations for the future is to leverage my skills and experiences to create positive social impact, particularly in areas such as education, technology, and environmental sustainability. By contributing to society, I hope to honour the values and lessons from Kerala and inspire others to do the same.

Personal Reflections

Reflecting on my journey, the lessons from Kerala's rich heritage and traditions have profoundly shaped my outlook on life and work. The cultural values of integrity, empathy, adaptability, and collaboration have guided my personal and professional growth, while the emphasis on balancing tradition and modernity has inspired my vision for the future.

These lessons have taught me the importance of staying true to one's values and maintaining a positive and resilient mindset in the face of challenges. They have also reinforced the power of community and the impact of collective efforts in achieving shared goals. As I continue on my journey, I am grateful for the wisdom and insights gained from Kerala's vibrant culture and traditions, which have been instrumental in shaping my path and guiding me toward a fulfilling and purposeful life.

In conclusion, the lessons from Kerala's rich heritage and traditions have shaped my outlook on life and work, guiding my personal values, professional growth, and vision for the future. These lessons have instilled in me a deep appreciation for integrity, empathy, adaptability, and collaboration, and have inspired a commitment to contributing positively to society. As I continue on my journey, I am grateful for the wisdom and insights gained from Kerala's vibrant culture, which have been instrumental in shaping my path and guiding me toward a fulfilling and purposeful life.

CHAPTER THREE

BANGALORE: THE SILICON VALLEY OF INDIA

Bangalore, often hailed as the Silicon Valley of India, holds a special place in my journey of personal and professional growth. Renowned for its dynamic tech industry, vibrant cultural scene, and cosmopolitan charm, Bangalore has shaped my experiences, aspirations, and perspectives in profound ways. In this chapter, we delve into how Bangalore's unique attributes have influenced my career trajectory, entrepreneurial spirit, and cultural immersion.

Bangalore's Tech Scene and Personal Growth

Bangalore's transformation into India's tech hub, often referred to as the "Silicon Valley of India," is a tale of strategic evolution and visionary growth. Historically, Bangalore was known for its pleasant climate and lush greenery, attracting retirees and pensioners. However, its metamorphosis began in the late 20th century, driven by a confluence of factors including policy reforms, educational excellence, and entrepreneurial spirit.

The roots of Bangalore's tech industry can be traced back to the establishment of public sector undertakings such as Hindustan Aeronautics Limited (HAL) and Indian Space Research Organisation (ISRO) in the 1960s and 1970s. These organizations fostered a culture of engineering and technological innovation. The pivotal moment came in the 1980s and 1990s when economic liberalization policies opened India to global markets.

Bangalore became a magnet for foreign investment, attracting multinational corporations like IBM, Texas Instruments, and Infosys, which chose the city as their operational base.

The presence of major players like Wipro, Infosys, and Tata Consultancy Services (TCS) catalysed Bangalore's tech boom. These companies not only generated employment but also inspired a wave of start-ups, turning the city into a hotbed for entrepreneurship. The software services sector thrived, with Bangalore's skilled workforce offering cost-effective solutions to global clients. The city's growth was further accelerated by the establishment of the International Tech Park Bangalore (ITPB) in Whitefield and the Electronics City, housing numerous IT companies.

Today, Bangalore's tech landscape is characterized by its vibrant ecosystem of start-ups, established giants, and research institutions. The city has evolved into a dynamic hub for innovation, attracting talent from across India and the world. Its tech parks and innovation centres buzz with creativity and ambition, fostering an environment where ideas flourish and technology drives progress.

Opportunities for Personal and Professional Development

Bangalore's tech scene offers a plethora of opportunities for personal and professional growth, making it an ideal destination for aspiring techies and entrepreneurs. The city's diverse and competitive environment fosters skill enhancement, career advancement, and personal development.

One of the most significant advantages of working in Bangalore's tech industry is the access to cutting-edge technologies and projects. Professionals in the city have the opportunity to work on global-scale initiatives, collaborate with leading experts, and gain exposure to the latest advancements in technology. This exposure not only enhances technical skills but also nurtures problem-solving abilities and innovative thinking.

The city's tech ecosystem is also known for its emphasis on continuous learning and skill development. Many companies offer training programs, workshops, and certifications to help employees stay updated with industry trends. Additionally, Bangalore hosts numerous tech conferences, hackathons, and seminars, providing platforms for networking, knowledge exchange, and skill refinement.

Networking and collaboration play a pivotal role in personal development in Bangalore. The city's vibrant tech community encourages professionals to connect with peers, mentors, and industry leaders. These connections open doors to new opportunities, collaborations, and partnerships. Attending meetups, tech events, and industry gatherings enables individuals to expand their professional networks and gain insights from experienced professionals.

For me, transitioning from the serene landscapes of Kerala to the bustling tech environment of Bangalore was transformative. The shift was both thrilling and challenging, offering me numerous opportunities to learn and grow. In Bangalore, I found myself surrounded by a dynamic mix of cultures, ideas, and aspirations. This diversity enriched my perspective, teaching me to appreciate different viewpoints and embrace new challenges with an open mind.

Influence on Lifestyle and Mindset

Living and working in Bangalore's tech-driven environment has a profound impact on lifestyle and mindset. The city's fast-paced, innovative culture encourages individuals to adapt quickly, embrace change, and foster a growth-oriented mindset.

One of the defining aspects of Bangalore is its cultural diversity. The city is a melting pot of people from different states, countries, and backgrounds. This diversity not only enriches the cultural fabric of Bangalore but also offers individuals the opportunity to interact with a wide range of perspectives and ideas. For someone like me, who grew up in Kerala with its own rich traditions and values, Bangalore's multicultural environment provided a broader canvas to understand and appreciate different cultures.

The tech scene in Bangalore is characterized by its dynamism and rapid pace of change. This environment encourages individuals to be adaptable and resilient. The ability to embrace change, learn new skills, and innovate is crucial for success in this competitive landscape. Professionals in Bangalore are constantly exposed to new challenges, technologies, and business models, fostering a mindset that thrives on problem-solving and continuous improvement.

My experience in Bangalore taught me the value of adaptability and resilience. The fast-paced nature of the tech industry demanded quick thinking and the ability to navigate through uncertainties. This mindset not only helped me in my professional endeavours but also instilled a sense of confidence and determination in my personal life.

Furthermore, Bangalore's tech culture emphasizes work-life balance and well-being. The city offers a range of recreational activities, wellness centres, and green spaces that promote relaxation and rejuvenation. Professionals in Bangalore are encouraged to prioritize self-care, maintain a healthy work-life balance, and engage in activities that nurture physical and mental well-being.

In conclusion, Bangalore's tech scene has a profound impact on personal growth and mindset. The city's evolution into a tech hub offers individuals opportunities for career advancement, skill enhancement, and personal development. The dynamic environment encourages adaptability, resilience, and a growth-oriented mindset. The cultural diversity and emphasis on work-life balance further contribute to a holistic approach to personal and professional success. For me, the journey from Kerala to Bangalore has been transformative, enriching my life with valuable experiences, insights, and opportunities for growth.

Balancing Tech Life with Positivity

Managing Stress and Burnout

Navigating the fast-paced tech world often feels like walking a tightrope. The demands of the industry—tight deadlines, high-stakes projects, and constant innovation—can easily lead to stress and burnout. Early in my career, I encountered these pressures head-on, and they taught me valuable lessons about managing stress and preserving mental well-being.

Identifying stressors is the first step toward managing them effectively. In the tech industry, common stressors include project deadlines, long working hours, and the need for continuous learning and adaptation. The pressure to keep up with rapid technological advancements and maintain high performance can sometimes feel overwhelming. I remember a particularly intense period early in my career as a network technician, where a critical system failure required working around the clock to restore services. The relentless pace was physically and mentally draining, but it was also a learning experience in how to manage stress.

To address stress and prevent burnout, I adopted several strategies that proved beneficial. One of the most effective techniques was time management. Breaking down tasks into manageable chunks and setting realistic deadlines helped alleviate the pressure. Additionally, incorporating regular breaks into the workday allowed me to recharge and maintain focus. I also found that mindfulness practices, such as meditation and deep-breathing exercises, were instrumental in reducing stress. These techniques helped me stay grounded and manage anxiety, even during the most demanding times.

Another crucial aspect of stress management is seeking support when needed. Building a network of colleagues, mentors, and friends who can offer advice and encouragement was invaluable. During high-pressure situations, having someone to share experiences and solutions with provided a much-needed sense of camaraderie and relief.

Cultivating a Positive Work-Life Balance

In the tech industry, maintaining a positive work-life balance is essential for long-term success and personal well-being. The line between work and personal life can easily blur, especially in a field where the pace is relentless and the stakes are high. From my own experience, setting boundaries and prioritizing self-care became key elements in achieving a balance that supported both professional success and personal happiness.

Setting clear boundaries between work and personal life is vital. In the early stages of my career, I struggled with this balance, often finding myself working late into the night and bringing work home on weekends. However, over time, I learned the importance of establishing limits. Creating a defined work schedule and sticking to it helped me maintain a sense of normalcy and prevent burnout. I also made it a point to communicate these boundaries with my team and supervisors, which fostered a mutual understanding and respect for personal time.

Prioritizing self-care was another crucial aspect of maintaining balance. Engaging in regular physical exercise, such as jogging or playing sports, provided a much-needed outlet for stress and contributed to overall well-being. I also made time for hobbies and activities that brought joy and relaxation, whether it was exploring Bangalore's cultural scene or indulging in cooking, which was a passion I had cultivated since my days in Kerala.

Additionally, finding moments for relaxation and reflection was essential. Whether it was through reading, meditation, or simply spending time with loved ones, these activities helped me recharge and maintain a positive outlook. Creating a dedicated space for relaxation and unwinding at home also played a significant role in achieving a balanced lifestyle.

Strategies for Maintaining a Positive Mindset

Maintaining a positive mindset in the fast-paced tech world is crucial for both personal satisfaction and professional success. Developing positive thinking practices and setting clear goals are effective strategies to foster a resilient and optimistic outlook.

One of the most impactful positive thinking practices is gratitude. Taking time each day to acknowledge and appreciate the positive aspects of life—whether it's personal achievements, supportive colleagues, or small victories—can shift focus from stressors to the positive elements. I found that starting or ending my day with a moment of gratitude helped maintain a balanced perspective and reinforced a sense of accomplishment.

Visualization techniques also played a significant role in maintaining a positive mindset. Setting clear personal and professional goals, and visualizing the steps needed to achieve them, created a sense of purpose and motivation. For instance, when leading a team as an IT infrastructure manager, I used visualization to plan and execute projects successfully. By envisioning the desired outcomes and the path to reach them, I was able to stay focused and overcome obstacles with confidence.

Furthermore, fostering a supportive environment both at work and home contributed to a positive mindset. Building strong relationships with colleagues and friends created a network of encouragement and mutual support. Engaging in collaborative projects and celebrating team successes reinforced a positive and cohesive work culture.

Reflecting on my journey from Kerala to Bangalore, I realize how these strategies helped me navigate the complexities of the tech industry. The cultural values instilled in me during my formative years, such as community spirit and resilience, complemented the positive thinking practices I adopted in my career. The blend of traditional values and modern techniques created a foundation for personal growth and success.

In conclusion, balancing the fast-paced tech world with a positive mindset requires a combination of effective stress management, work-life balance, and positive thinking strategies. By identifying stressors, setting boundaries, and prioritizing self-care, individuals can maintain their well-being and thrive in a demanding environment. Positive thinking practices and goal-setting further enhance resilience and motivation, contributing to long-term success and fulfilment. My experiences in both Kerala and Bangalore have taught me the importance of these strategies, shaping my approach to life and work in meaningful ways.

Stories of Resilience and Success from Bangalore's Tech Community

Overcoming Challenges

Bangalore's tech scene is a tapestry woven with stories of perseverance and triumph. My own journey mirrors the resilience and determination that characterize many in this vibrant city. Early in my career, I encountered challenges that seemed insurmountable, yet these obstacles became valuable lessons in perseverance and growth.

One personal anecdote that stands out is from my days as a network technician. I was part of a team handling a major network upgrade for a large client. The project was crucial, with tight deadlines and high expectations. Midway through the upgrade, we faced an unexpected hardware failure that threatened to derail the entire project. The stress was palpable, and the pressure to deliver on time was immense.

Despite the setback, maintaining a positive mindset was crucial. We convened a brainstorming session, focusing on solutions rather than dwelling on the problem. By leveraging the collective expertise of the team, we quickly identified an alternative approach that allowed us to get the project back on track. The experience taught me that resilience isn't just about enduring hardship but about staying focused and adaptable in the face of adversity.

This story is reflective of a broader trend within Bangalore's tech community. Many individuals have faced significant hurdles in their careers, from startup failures to product delays. One notable example is the story of a local entrepreneur who started a tech startup that initially struggled with market fit and funding challenges. However, through relentless perseverance and adaptability, the startup pivoted to a new model that resonated with a broader audience. Today, it's a successful player in the tech space, illustrating that setbacks can often be the prelude to greater achievements.

The lesson learned from these experiences is that overcoming challenges often requires a blend of positive thinking, adaptability, and collaboration. By focusing on solutions and maintaining a resilient attitude, individuals can navigate the complexities of the tech industry and turn obstacles into opportunities.

Innovations and Breakthroughs

Bangalore's reputation as the Silicon Valley of India is built on a foundation of innovation and technological breakthroughs. The city has been the birthplace of numerous successful projects that have significantly impacted the tech landscape, both locally and globally.

One prominent example is the development of a leading-edge fintech platform that originated in Bangalore. This platform, which started as a small startup, faced numerous technical and regulatory challenges. However, through a combination of innovative problem-solving and a commitment to excellence, the team developed a solution that revolutionized digital payments in India. The success of this platform not only demonstrated Bangalore's prowess in fintech but also contributed to the broader adoption of digital financial services across the country.

Another inspiring story is that of a tech company that created a groundbreaking artificial intelligence (AI) solution for healthcare diagnostics. This project faced initial skepticism and technical difficulties but eventually delivered a tool that significantly improved diagnostic accuracy and efficiency. The impact on the healthcare industry has been profound, with the solution being adopted by hospitals and clinics worldwide. This innovation highlights how Bangalore's tech community is at the forefront of developing technologies that address real-world problems.

These success stories underscore the city's role as a hub of technological advancement. They reflect a culture of continuous innovation, where challenges are met with creative solutions and where breakthroughs are driven by a combination of expertise, perseverance, and a willingness to push the boundaries of what's possible.

Building a Supportive Community

The strength of Bangalore's tech community lies not only in its individual achievements but also in its collaborative spirit. Building a supportive network is crucial for fostering success and resilience, and mentorship plays a significant role in this ecosystem.

One of the most impactful experiences in my career was the mentorship I received from seasoned professionals. Early on, I was fortunate to be guided by mentors who shared their wisdom and provided valuable insights into navigating the tech industry. Their support was instrumental in helping me develop the skills and confidence needed to advance in my career. The importance of mentorship in Bangalore's tech scene cannot be overstated, as it provides emerging professionals with the guidance and encouragement needed to thrive.

Additionally, collaborative initiatives and community-driven projects are a testament to the supportive nature of Bangalore's tech ecosystem. For instance, numerous tech meetups, hackathons, and industry conferences are held regularly, providing platforms for professionals to connect, share ideas, and collaborate on projects. These events foster a sense of community and create opportunities for individuals to learn from one another and contribute to collective success.

One notable example is a tech incubator in Bangalore that supports early-stage startups through mentorship, funding, and networking opportunities. This incubator has played a pivotal role in nurturing new talent and facilitating the growth of innovative startups. The collaborative environment within the incubator encourages knowledge sharing and fosters a culture of mutual support, which is essential for the success of emerging entrepreneurs.

Reflecting on my experiences from Kerala to Bangalore, I've seen how the values of community and support play a crucial role in shaping successful careers. The sense of camaraderie and shared purpose within the tech community is akin to the community spirit I experienced growing up in Kalliassery. Just as local cultural events and festivals fostered a sense of belonging and collaboration in my village, the tech community in Bangalore thrives on collective effort and mutual support.

In summary, the stories of resilience and success from Bangalore's tech community highlight the importance of overcoming challenges, fostering innovation, and building a supportive network. Through personal anecdotes and examples of ground-breaking projects, we see how the city's tech scene is characterized by perseverance, creativity, and collaboration. These elements contribute to a vibrant and dynamic ecosystem that drives both personal and professional growth.

Conclusion

This Chapter has provided an insightful exploration into Bangalore, often hailed as the Silicon Valley of India, and its profound impact on personal growth within the tech industry. Bangalore's vibrant tech scene has served as a catalyst for innovation, entrepreneurship, and career opportunities, shaping the professional journeys of countless individuals.

The tech scene in Bangalore is characterized by its dynamism, diversity, and entrepreneurial spirit. Professionals in this ecosystem benefit from exposure to cutting-edge technologies, collaborative work environments, and a culture that values creativity and innovation. These factors contribute significantly to personal and professional development, fostering a mindset of continuous learning and adaptation.

Balancing the fast-paced tech world with a positive mindset requires resilience, adaptability, and a proactive approach to professional growth. The stories of resilience and success from Bangalore's tech community illustrate how individuals have navigated challenges, capitalized on opportunities, and emerged stronger and more accomplished.

In conclusion, Bangalore's tech ecosystem offers a fertile ground for personal and professional growth, providing individuals with the tools, resources, and opportunities to thrive. By embracing its innovative spirit and fostering a positive mindset, professionals can leverage Bangalore's dynamic landscape to achieve their career aspirations and contribute meaningfully to the global tech industry.

OVERCOMING CHALLENGES

Challenges are an inevitable part of any journey, especially in the dynamic and fast-paced world of technology. In this chapter, we explore the diverse challenges faced by individuals and organizations within Bangalore's tech community, highlighting strategies for resilience, innovation, and growth amidst adversity.

Facing Common Tech Industry Challenges

Rapid Technological Advancements

In the tech industry, rapid technological advancements are both a thrilling and daunting reality. The pace at which new technologies emerge can sometimes feel overwhelming, and staying ahead of the curve requires more than just keeping up—it demands a proactive and strategic approach.

Keeping Up with Innovation

The constant evolution of technology means that yesterday's cutting-edge solutions quickly become today's obsolete tools. For someone in the tech field, this can create a perpetual sense of urgency. During my early years in the industry, I vividly recall the moment when the shift from traditional desktop support to cloud-based solutions was in full swing. It was a challenge to transition from maintaining physical servers to managing virtual environments and cloud services. At that time, I made a conscious decision to embrace change rather than resist it. I started dedicating a portion of my weekly schedule to learning about emerging technologies.

This included subscribing to tech journals, attending webinars, and joining online forums.

The key strategy here is to embed learning into your routine. Make it a habit to regularly update your skillset and knowledge base. For instance, leveraging platforms like Coursera or LinkedIn Learning for short courses on the latest technologies can be immensely beneficial. Networking with peers and participating in industry meetups also provides exposure to new tools and practices. By making learning a continuous process, you not only stay relevant but also position yourself as a knowledgeable resource within your team.

Continuous Learning

Continuous education is not merely about staying current with technology; it's about fostering a mindset that is open to growth and adaptation. When I transitioned from a network technician to a systems administrator, I faced the daunting task of understanding new infrastructure components and their integration. This shift was not just about acquiring new technical skills but also about adapting to a new way of thinking.

Engaging in continuous learning means embracing opportunities for professional development. Certifications, advanced degrees, or even self-study through online resources can help bridge knowledge gaps. Furthermore, learning from colleagues and mentors can offer valuable insights and practical advice that is often not covered in formal training. The goal is to build a habit of curiosity and self-improvement, making learning an integral part of your career development.

Managing Workload and Deadlines

The tech industry is renowned for its high-pressure environment, where tight deadlines and heavy workloads are common. Balancing the demands of the job while maintaining your well-being requires effective strategies and techniques.

High-pressure Environments

Navigating high-pressure environments can be particularly challenging. Early in my career, I was often involved in urgent projects that required immediate attention and quick turnarounds. One specific instance involved a critical system outage during a major product launch. The pressure to resolve the issue swiftly was immense, and it tested my ability to manage stress.

In such situations, it's crucial to maintain a level-headed approach. Techniques like breaking down tasks into smaller, manageable segments and focusing on one thing at a time can be incredibly effective. Stress management techniques, such as deep breathing exercises and short breaks, can also help in maintaining focus and composure. Developing a strong support network within your team can also provide encouragement and assistance during high-pressure periods.

Effective Time Management

Effective time management is another essential skill for handling workload and deadlines. One technique that proved invaluable in my career was the implementation of time-blocking. This method involves allocating specific blocks of time to different tasks or projects. By doing so, you can ensure that each task receives the attention it needs without feeling overwhelmed by competing priorities.

Additionally, prioritizing tasks based on their urgency and importance can help in managing workloads efficiently. Utilizing tools like task management software or to-do lists can aid in keeping track of deadlines and progress. Regularly reviewing and adjusting your priorities based on changing circumstances can also enhance your ability to meet deadlines effectively.

Navigating Workplace Dynamics

The dynamics of workplace interactions can significantly impact your career experience. Building effective relationships with colleagues and managing conflicts are crucial for fostering a positive work environment.

Team Collaboration and Communication

Team collaboration and communication are key elements of a successful tech project. From my experience, I found that fostering an environment of open communication and mutual respect is vital. During a major infrastructure upgrade project, effective communication within the team helped in coordinating efforts and resolving issues promptly.

To enhance team collaboration, consider implementing practices such as regular team meetings, clear project documentation, and feedback sessions. Encouraging an environment where team members feel comfortable sharing ideas and concerns can lead to more innovative solutions and a stronger team dynamic.

Handling Conflicts

Conflicts are inevitable in any work environment, but how you handle them can make a significant difference. I recall a period when a disagreement over project priorities created tension within the team. Addressing conflicts promptly and professionally is crucial. I found that approaching conflicts with empathy and seeking to understand different perspectives helped in finding common ground.

Implementing conflict resolution strategies, such as active listening and finding compromise, can help in maintaining a positive work environment. It's important to address conflicts constructively and focus on finding solutions that benefit the team as a whole.

Dealing with Job Uncertainty and Career Transitions

Job uncertainty and career transitions are common in the tech industry, given its dynamic nature. Navigating these changes effectively requires resilience and a proactive approach.

Adapting to Change

The ability to adapt to change is crucial for career longevity. My transition from a network technician to a systems administrator was a significant change, requiring adaptation to new roles and responsibilities. Embracing change involves staying open to new opportunities and being willing to step out of your comfort zone.

Developing a mindset that views change as an opportunity for growth can help in navigating career transitions. Seeking mentorship and advice from experienced professionals can also provide valuable guidance during periods of uncertainty. It's important to remain flexible and proactive in exploring new avenues for career development.

Building Resilience

Building resilience is essential for maintaining motivation and positivity during challenging times. One strategy I found effective was setting short-term goals to stay focused and motivated. Celebrating small achievements and recognizing progress, even during difficult periods, can help in maintaining a positive outlook.

Additionally, developing a strong support network of colleagues, mentors, and friends can provide encouragement and perspective during career transitions. Engaging in self-care practices and maintaining a work-life balance can also contribute to overall resilience and well-being.

In summary, the tech industry presents a range of challenges that require proactive strategies and a positive mindset to overcome. By staying current with technological advancements, managing workload effectively, navigating workplace dynamics, and adapting to change, you can build a successful and fulfilling career in the ever-evolving tech landscape.

Overcoming Professional and Personal Hurdles

Throughout my journey in the tech industry, I have encountered numerous challenges—both professional and personal—that tested my resilience, determination, and adaptability. These experiences have shaped my growth, taught valuable lessons, and ultimately strengthened my resolve to overcome obstacles and achieve success. In this section, I share personal anecdotes of navigating hurdles, learning from setbacks, and embracing opportunities for growth.

Early Career Setbacks

In the early days of my career in the tech industry, I faced numerous challenges that seemed insurmountable at times. My journey began as a Technical Support Executive, where the sheer volume of issues and the constant need for quick resolutions tested my resolve. One particular instance stands out. I was handling a critical system outage for a major client—a problem that was beyond my initial scope of training. The pressure was immense, and I felt overwhelmed by the complexity of the issue.

Rather than succumbing to stress, I chose to approach the problem methodically. I reached out to more experienced colleagues, absorbing their advice and strategies. This collaborative approach not only helped resolve the issue but also taught me the value of seeking help and learning from others. This experience was a powerful lesson in resilience. It highlighted the importance of perseverance and the willingness to learn continuously. From this setback, I learned that challenges, while daunting, offer valuable learning experiences and opportunities for growth.

Major Project Failures

As I progressed in my career, I took on larger responsibilities, including leading projects as a Network Operations Center (NOC) team leader. One notable failure was a project aimed at overhauling a client's entire IT infrastructure. Despite meticulous planning, the project faced numerous issues during implementation, leading to significant delays and client dissatisfaction.

Initially, the failure felt like a personal defeat. However, I quickly realized that this setback could be transformed into a learning experience. I organized a series of post-mortem meetings with my team to analyse what went wrong and identify areas for improvement. This process of reflection and analysis was crucial in understanding the root causes of the failure and devising strategies to avoid similar issues in the future.

The lessons learned from this project were invaluable. They not only improved my project management skills but also reinforced the importance of adaptability and thorough preparation. Failure, while painful, can provide deep insights and pave the way for future successes if approached with the right mindset.

Balancing Personal Life and Professional Demands

Balancing personal life with demanding professional responsibilities has been one of the most challenging aspects of my career. During a particularly intense period, I was managing multiple high-stakes projects while also dealing with personal issues back in Kerala. The strain of juggling these responsibilities took a toll on my well-being.

To navigate this challenging period, I implemented several strategies to maintain balance. I learned to set clear boundaries between work and personal life, ensuring that I allocated time for self-care and family. I also found solace in the cultural practices I grew up with—participating in festivals and community events provided a much-needed respite and kept me grounded.

Additionally, I began to prioritize tasks more effectively, using time management techniques such as setting specific goals and breaking tasks into manageable segments. This approach not only improved my productivity but also helped me maintain a sense of control over my work and personal life. Balancing these demands required conscious effort, but it taught me the importance of maintaining equilibrium to sustain long-term success.

Mentorship and Support

Throughout my career, mentorship has played a crucial role in overcoming professional and personal hurdles. Early in my career, I was fortunate to have mentors who provided guidance and support during challenging times. One mentor, in particular, had a profound impact on my approach to overcoming obstacles. Their advice on maintaining a positive mindset and focusing on long-term goals helped me navigate several tough situations.

Building a support network was equally important. I actively sought out connections within the tech industry and participated in professional groups and forums. These connections provided not only career advice but also emotional support during difficult times. By surrounding myself with a network of supportive peers and mentors, I was able to draw strength and perspective from their experiences.

Mentorship and support networks have taught me that overcoming challenges is not a solitary journey. By engaging with others and seeking guidance, we can gain valuable insights and encouragement that make navigating obstacles more manageable. Building and nurturing these relationships has been instrumental in my career growth and personal development.

In conclusion, my techie life has been marked by various challenges, from early career setbacks to major project failures and the struggle to balance personal and professional demands. Each experience has provided valuable lessons and insights, shaping my approach to overcoming hurdles and maintaining a positive mindset. By embracing these lessons and leveraging the support of mentors and peers, I have learned to navigate the complexities of the tech world while staying resilient and focused on long-term success.

Techniques to Stay Positive During Tough Times

Developing a Resilient Mindset

The journey through tough times is rarely smooth, but cultivating a resilient mindset can significantly ease the way. Resilience isn't about avoiding challenges but about developing the mental toughness to confront and overcome them. This skill has been crucial throughout my career, especially when faced with high-pressure situations and setbacks.

One technique that has consistently helped me maintain a positive outlook during difficult periods is practicing positive thinking. This involves consciously focusing on the positive aspects of a situation, rather than dwelling on negatives. For example, during a particularly challenging project where I felt overwhelmed by the scope and deadlines, I made it a habit to start each day by reflecting on what I had achieved rather than what was still pending. This shift in perspective helped me approach the day with a sense of accomplishment and motivated me to tackle the remaining tasks with renewed energy.

Building resilience is another key aspect of staying positive. Resilience can be strengthened through various methods, including embracing challenges as opportunities for growth and maintaining flexibility in the face of change. One instance from my career that highlights this involved a major systems overhaul project that initially faced numerous setbacks. Instead of viewing these setbacks as failures, I chose to see them as learning experiences. This mindset not only helped me recover more swiftly but also allowed me to adapt more effectively to unforeseen challenges.

Practical Stress Management

Managing stress is essential for maintaining a positive mindset, and there are several effective techniques to do so. Mindfulness and relaxation practices are particularly useful for navigating stressful periods. Incorporating mindfulness into my daily routine has been incredibly beneficial. Simple practices, such as mindful breathing and meditation, help center my thoughts and reduce anxiety. For example, during high-stress periods in my career, I began dedicating ten minutes each morning to mindfulness meditation. This practice helped me start the day with a clearer, more focused mind and better equipped me to handle stress throughout the day.

Physical well-being also plays a crucial role in maintaining mental health. Regular exercise and a balanced diet have been instrumental in managing stress. When working long hours or handling intense projects, it's easy to neglect physical health. However, I found that integrating physical activity into my routine—whether through jogging, yoga, or even a simple walk—provided a necessary break and helped clear my mind. Additionally, maintaining a nutritious diet helped sustain my energy levels and kept my mood stable, which in turn positively impacted my approach to challenges.

Goal Setting and Motivation

Setting and achieving realistic goals is another technique that can help maintain motivation and positivity. Goal setting provides direction and a sense of purpose, which is especially important during challenging times. In my experience, breaking down larger goals into smaller, manageable tasks has been particularly effective. For example, during a complex project, instead of focusing on the end goal, I broke it down into smaller milestones. This approach allowed me to focus on one step at a time, celebrate small victories, and maintain momentum.

Celebrating small wins is also crucial for boosting morale. Acknowledging and appreciating minor achievements keeps motivation high and reinforces a positive mindset. I recall a time when a major client project faced significant delays. Despite the setbacks, every time we completed a milestone—no matter how small—I made it a point to celebrate with my team. These celebrations, whether through a simple thank-you or a small team gathering, helped keep the team's spirits high and fostered a sense of accomplishment and progress.

Seeking Support and Resources

Seeking support and utilizing available resources is an important aspect of maintaining a positive mindset. Professional help, such as counseling or coaching, can provide valuable perspectives and strategies for managing stress and overcoming obstacles. Early in my career, when I faced particularly challenging periods, I sought guidance from mentors and professional coaches. Their advice and support were instrumental in helping me navigate tough situations and maintain a positive outlook.

Building a support system of peers, mentors, and professionals is another effective strategy. Engaging with a network of supportive individuals provides not only practical advice but also emotional encouragement. Throughout my career, I have been fortunate to have mentors who offered guidance and support during difficult times. For instance, during a particularly challenging project, one of my mentors helped me reframe my approach to the problem and provided strategies for managing stress. This support was invaluable in helping me stay focused and positive.

Creating and nurturing a support system requires intentional effort. Engaging in professional networks, participating in industry events, and actively seeking out mentors can help build a strong network of support. Additionally, being open to offering support to others in your network can create a reciprocal environment of mutual encouragement and assistance.

In summary, staying positive during tough times involves developing a resilient mindset, managing stress effectively, setting and achieving goals, and seeking support from professional resources and personal networks. Drawing from my experiences in both Kerala and my tech career, these techniques have proven invaluable in maintaining a positive outlook and navigating the challenges of both personal and professional life. By incorporating these strategies, individuals can build resilience, enhance well-being, and foster a more positive approach to overcoming obstacles.

Conclusion

Chapter 4 has explored the theme of overcoming challenges in the tech industry, highlighting both common hurdles and effective strategies for facing them. In the fast-paced and rapidly evolving world of technology, professionals often encounter obstacles that require resilience, adaptability, and innovative thinking to overcome.

By acknowledging and addressing common challenges such as technological disruptions, resource constraints, and competitive pressures, individuals can develop proactive approaches to mitigate risks and seize opportunities. Strategies discussed include fostering a culture of continuous learning, embracing technological advancements, and nurturing a supportive work environment.

Personal anecdotes of overcoming professional and personal hurdles illustrate the transformative power of perseverance and strategic decision-making in navigating challenges. These stories underscore the importance of resilience, collaboration, and a positive mindset in achieving sustained success in the tech industry.

In conclusion, while challenges are inevitable, they also present opportunities for growth and innovation. By equipping oneself with the right mindset, skills, and support network, individuals can not only overcome obstacles but also thrive in a dynamic and competitive tech landscape

CHAPTER FIVE

SETTING AND ACHIEVING GOALS

In the fast-paced world of technology, setting and achieving goals is crucial to success. For me, this journey began in the small village of Kalliassery in Kerala, where I learned the importance of clarity, alignment with values, and consistent evaluation in goal setting. These principles have guided me throughout my career, from my early days in the tech industry to my current role in leadership.

Importance of Setting Clear, Achievable Goals

Setting clear, achievable goals is a cornerstone of personal and professional success. Goals provide a roadmap for the future, guiding actions, decisions, and efforts toward desired outcomes. In this section, we delve into the significance of goal setting, examining its impact on motivation, focus, productivity, and overall well-being.

Defining Clear Goals

Understanding the importance of clarity in goal setting was a lesson I learned early in life. Growing up in Kerala, I participated in many cultural programs and sports events. Whether it was organizing a local football tournament or planning a cultural festival, the importance of clear, specific goals was evident. If our team didn't have a clear understanding of what success looked like, we would struggle to coordinate our efforts and often fall short of our objectives.

In the tech industry, clarity remains crucial. Vague goals can lead to confusion and misalignment, wasting time and resources. When I transitioned from a technical support role to network administration, I realized how critical it was to set specific goals for my professional growth. For instance, rather than setting a vague goal like "improve my networking skills," I focused on obtaining a specific certification within a set timeframe. This clear goal allowed me to create a structured study plan, seek resources, and measure my progress effectively.

Breaking down complex goals into manageable steps is another aspect of clarity that cannot be overstated. In the tech world, where projects often involve intricate systems and numerous stakeholders, a large, ambiguous goal can be overwhelming. During my time as a systems administrator, I was tasked with a major project to upgrade our company's IT infrastructure. Initially, the project's complexity was daunting, but by breaking it down into smaller, actionable steps, we were able to make consistent progress. We tackled each component methodically, from hardware procurement to software installation, which allowed us to maintain momentum and stay on track.

Aligning Goals with Personal and Professional Values

As I advanced in my career, I realized the importance of aligning goals with my personal and professional values. In Kerala, family and community played a central role in shaping my values. I learned to prioritize integrity, empathy, and a strong work ethic. These values have guided my approach to goal setting throughout my career.

Values-driven goals are not only more motivating but also more sustainable. When your goals reflect your core beliefs, you are more likely to stay committed, even when faced with obstacles. During a challenging period in my career, I faced a decision about whether to take on a project that conflicted with my values. The project promised financial gain, but it involved practices that went against my ethical standards. By choosing to align my goals with my values, I was able to maintain my integrity and ultimately found a path that was both ethically sound and professionally rewarding.

Prioritization is another critical aspect of aligning goals with long-term visions. In the tech industry, it's easy to get caught up in the urgency of short-term demands and lose sight of broader aspirations. To avoid this, I regularly reassess my goals, ensuring they are aligned with my long-term vision. For example, while working as a network technician, I set a goal to transition into leadership roles. This long-term vision guided my decisions and actions, helping me prioritize tasks that contributed to my development as a leader.

Measuring Progress and Success

Measuring progress and success is essential for staying on track and making necessary adjustments. During my early career in Kerala, participating in sports taught me the importance of tracking progress. Whether it was improving my performance in cricket or achieving fitness goals, I learned to set benchmarks and evaluate my achievements regularly.

In the tech industry, establishing metrics is crucial for assessing progress. When leading a project to develop a new software solution, we defined specific metrics to measure success, such as completion timelines, quality standards, and user satisfaction levels. These benchmarks provided a clear framework for evaluating our progress and identifying areas for improvement.

Evaluating outcomes and making necessary adjustments is a continuous process. In a rapidly changing industry, flexibility is key. When leading a team in Bangalore, we faced unexpected challenges that required us to adapt our goals and strategies. By regularly reviewing our progress and outcomes, we were able to pivot when necessary and keep the project on track. This iterative approach not only improved our chances of success but also enhanced our resilience and adaptability.

In Conclusion, Setting and achieving goals is a dynamic process that requires clarity, alignment with values, and consistent evaluation. My experiences in Kerala and the tech industry have taught me the importance of defining clear goals, aligning them with personal and professional values, and measuring progress effectively. These principles have guided me throughout my career, helping me navigate challenges and seize opportunities for growth.

In the fast-paced world of technology, the ability to set and achieve goals is a critical skill that can propel individuals and organizations toward success. By understanding the importance of clarity, aligning goals with values, and consistently evaluating progress, we can create a roadmap for achieving our aspirations and making a meaningful impact in our careers and communities. Whether in Kerala or Bangalore, the lessons of goal setting remain relevant and transformative, shaping our journey toward personal and professional fulfillment.

Strategies for Goal-Setting with a Positive Mindset

Setting goals with a positive mindset is a transformative process that can drive success and fulfillment. Throughout my journey from the serene landscapes of Kerala to the dynamic tech scene in Bangalore, I have learned the value of visualization, overcoming obstacles, and flexible planning. These strategies have been instrumental in shaping my career and personal life, enabling me to navigate challenges and achieve meaningful goals.

Visualization and Affirmation Techniques

Visualization and affirmations are powerful tools for cultivating a positive mindset and achieving goals. Growing up in Kerala, I was surrounded by natural beauty and vibrant culture, which inspired a sense of imagination and possibility. This environment nurtured my ability to visualize success, a skill that has been invaluable in my tech career.

Visualizing Success

The power of mental imagery in achieving goals cannot be overstated. Visualization involves creating a vivid mental image of the desired outcome, allowing you to see yourself succeeding. This technique helps build confidence and clarity, reinforcing your commitment to your goals.

When I transitioned from a network technician to a leadership role, visualization played a crucial role in my success. I would often picture myself leading teams, solving complex problems, and making impactful decisions. This mental rehearsal prepared me for the challenges I faced and instilled a sense of confidence in my abilities.

To effectively visualize success, it's essential to create a detailed mental image of your goals. Imagine the sights, sounds, and emotions associated with achieving your objectives. The more specific and vivid the imagery, the more powerful the impact on your mindset and motivation. This technique not only enhances your focus but also helps you identify the steps needed to achieve your goals.

Using Affirmations

Affirmations are positive statements that reinforce your beliefs and intentions. By regularly repeating affirmations, you can reprogram your subconscious mind to support your goals and aspirations.

In my early career, I faced moments of self-doubt and uncertainty. During these times, I relied on affirmations to boost my confidence and maintain a positive outlook. Simple phrases like "I am capable of overcoming challenges" and "I am constantly growing and improving" served as reminders of my potential and resilience.

To harness the power of affirmations, choose statements that resonate with your values and goals. Repeat them daily, preferably in front of a mirror or during moments of reflection. Over time, these affirmations will help you internalize positive beliefs and attitudes, reinforcing your commitment to achieving your goals.

Overcoming Obstacles and Staying Motivated

In the pursuit of goals, obstacles are inevitable. However, a positive mindset can help you navigate these challenges and maintain your motivation. My experiences in both Kerala and the tech industry have taught me the importance of resilience and determination in overcoming obstacles.

Identifying Barriers

Recognizing potential challenges is the first step in overcoming them. In the tech industry, projects often face unexpected hurdles, from technical glitches to resource constraints. By anticipating these challenges, you can develop strategies to address them effectively.

During my career as a systems administrator, I encountered numerous obstacles, such as tight deadlines and complex technical issues. To navigate these challenges, I adopted a proactive approach, identifying potential barriers early on and devising contingency plans. This preparation allowed me to stay focused and resilient, even in high-pressure situations.

To identify barriers, assess your goals and consider the factors that could hinder progress. This could include time constraints, resource limitations, or personal challenges. By acknowledging these obstacles, you can develop strategies to mitigate their impact and stay on track.

Sustaining Motivation

Maintaining enthusiasm and momentum is essential for achieving long-term goals. In the fast-paced tech world, it's easy to lose sight of your objectives amidst daily demands and pressures. However, a positive mindset can help you stay motivated and committed.

One technique for sustaining motivation is to celebrate small wins along the way. Recognizing and rewarding incremental progress reinforces your sense of achievement and fuels your determination to keep moving forward. In Kerala, where community and celebration are integral to the culture, I learned the value of acknowledging milestones, no matter how small.

Another strategy is to connect with your underlying purpose. Reflect on why your goals matter to you and how they align with your values and aspirations. This deeper connection can reignite your passion and drive, helping you stay focused on your long-term vision.

Flexible Planning and Adaptability

In an ever-changing world, flexibility and adaptability are key to successful goal-setting. My journey from Kerala to Bangalore has taught me the importance of embracing change and refining goals in response to evolving circumstances.

Embracing Change

Adapting goals in response to shifting circumstances is essential for staying relevant and resilient. In the tech industry, where innovation is constant, the ability to pivot and adjust goals is a valuable skill.

During my time as a network administrator, I encountered situations where project requirements changed unexpectedly. Instead of resisting these changes, I embraced them as opportunities for growth and learning. By remaining open to new possibilities, I was able to adapt my goals and strategies, ultimately achieving more than I initially envisioned.

To embrace change, cultivate a mindset of curiosity and flexibility. View challenges as opportunities for innovation and improvement, and be willing to adjust your goals as needed. This adaptability will enable you to navigate uncertainty and thrive in dynamic environments.

Iterative Goal-Setting

Continuous refinement and adjustment of goals are essential for improvement and growth. In Kerala, where traditional wisdom is often integrated with modern advancements, I learned the value of iterative progress and continuous learning.

In my tech career, I have adopted an iterative approach to goal-setting, regularly reviewing and refining my objectives. This process involves assessing my progress, identifying areas for improvement, and making necessary adjustments to stay aligned with my vision.

To practice iterative goal-setting, schedule regular check-ins to evaluate your progress and make adjustments as needed. Consider feedback from mentors and peers, and remain open to new insights and perspectives. This iterative process will help you stay adaptable and resilient, ensuring that your goals remain relevant and achievable.

In conclusion, setting and achieving goals with a positive mindset requires visualization, resilience, and adaptability. My experiences in Kerala and the tech industry have taught me the importance of visualizing success, overcoming obstacles, and embracing change. These strategies have empowered me to navigate challenges and achieve meaningful goals, both personally and professionally.

By incorporating visualization, affirmations, and flexible planning into your goal-setting process, you can cultivate a positive mindset and stay motivated in the face of challenges. Remember to celebrate small wins, connect with your underlying purpose, and remain open to new possibilities. With these strategies, you can achieve your goals and make a meaningful impact in your career and life.

Real-World Applications and Examples from My Tech Career

Drawing from my career journey—from a Technical Support Engineer to IT Head—illustrates how setting and achieving goals with a positive mindset can lead to significant accomplishments. Here, I share real-world applications and examples to highlight how these principles have been instrumental in my professional growth and success in the tech industry.

Early Career Goals and Achievements

When I first embarked on my tech career, my aspirations were modest yet ambitious. As someone who grew up in the nurturing environment of Kalliassery, Kerala, where community and collective progress were ingrained in daily life, I was eager to make a mark in the tech industry. My initial goals were centred around building a strong technical foundation and gaining industry experience, while also contributing to the projects I was part of.

Initial Aspirations

Entering the tech field as a network technician, I was enthusiastic about understanding the intricacies of networking and communication systems. My early career goals were focused on mastering technical skills and earning certifications that would validate my expertise. I vividly remember setting a goal to become proficient in network protocols and secure a certification within my first year.

Achieving this goal required discipline and dedication. I created a structured learning plan, dedicating time each day to study and practice. The pursuit of this goal taught me the importance of breaking down larger objectives into manageable tasks. I also realized the value of perseverance and consistency, as there were moments of doubt and fatigue that I had to overcome.

Learning from Successes

Securing my first certification was a pivotal moment that fuelled my confidence and motivated me to set higher goals. This achievement demonstrated the power of clear goal-setting and meticulous planning. It also instilled a sense of momentum that propelled me to take on more challenging projects. As I progressed in my career, I began to understand that each success was not just a milestone but a stepping stone towards greater accomplishments.

Reflecting on my early career successes, I learned the importance of celebrating achievements, no matter how small. These celebrations reinforced the positive impact of achieving goals and kept my motivation high. This approach has continued to guide me, reminding me that each goal achieved is a testament to my capabilities and a foundation for future growth.

Navigating Career Transitions

Career transitions are inevitable in the tech industry, where change is constant and new opportunities arise frequently. My journey from a network technician to leadership roles required a strategic recalibration of goals and a willingness to embrace change.

Adapting Goals

During career transitions, it became essential to reassess and adapt my goals to align with new roles and responsibilities. When I transitioned from a technical role to a managerial position, my objectives shifted from individual achievements to team leadership and project management. This transition required a different set of skills and a broader perspective on success.

Adapting goals involved identifying areas where I needed to grow and develop. I sought feedback from mentors and colleagues to gain insights into my strengths and areas for improvement. This feedback helped me tailor my goals to address the demands of my new role while leveraging my existing skills. I realized that flexibility and openness to learning were crucial in navigating transitions effectively.

Leveraging Opportunities

One of the key lessons from my career transitions was the importance of seizing unexpected opportunities. I remember a time when I was given the chance to lead a project that was outside my usual domain of expertise. Although initially daunting, I recognized it as an opportunity to expand my skill set and demonstrate my adaptability.

By aligning this opportunity with my personal goals of growth and development, I embraced the challenge with enthusiasm. I immersed myself in learning about the project's requirements and collaborated with experts in the field to ensure its success. This experience taught me that aligning unexpected opportunities with personal aspirations can lead to remarkable achievements and open doors to new possibilities.

Leading and Inspiring Teams

As my career progressed, I found immense fulfilment in leading teams and inspiring others to achieve their professional goals. This phase of my journey was influenced by the values of collaboration and community that I had learned in Kerala, where collective efforts were celebrated and supported.

Team-Based Goals

Setting collective goals for teams was a transformative experience that underscored the power of collaboration. I realized that when individuals are united by a common purpose, their collective energy and creativity can drive remarkable outcomes. In one of my leadership roles, I focused on creating a shared vision for the team, aligning individual goals with the overarching objectives of the organization.

By involving team members in the goal-setting process, I ensured that their perspectives and aspirations were considered. This approach fostered a sense of ownership and commitment, as team members felt connected to the goals they were working towards. Regular check-ins and open communication further strengthened this bond, allowing us to navigate challenges and celebrate achievements together.

Mentoring and Development

Mentorship played a pivotal role in my journey, both as a mentee and a mentor. In my early career, I benefited from the guidance of experienced professionals who provided valuable insights and encouragement. Their support inspired me to pay it forward by mentoring others and helping them achieve their goals.

As a mentor, I emphasized the importance of setting clear and achievable goals. I encouraged mentees to identify their strengths and passions, using them as a foundation for goal-setting. Through regular conversations and constructive feedback, I helped them navigate challenges and stay focused on their objectives.

One memorable mentoring experience involved guiding a junior team member who was unsure about the direction of their career. By listening to their aspirations and concerns, I helped them define a set of goals that aligned with their interests and strengths. Over time, I witnessed their growth and confidence blossom as they achieved each milestone, reaffirming the profound impact of mentorship.

Conclusion

My techie life, from its early stages in Kerala to leadership roles in Bangalore, has been defined by the practice of setting and achieving goals. Each phase of my career has brought unique challenges and opportunities, requiring adaptability, resilience, and a positive mindset.

Setting clear and achievable goals has been instrumental in shaping my career trajectory. The lessons learned from early successes and career transitions have provided valuable insights into the power of goal-setting. By aligning goals with personal values and embracing change, I have been able to navigate challenges and seize opportunities that have enriched my professional journey.

As a leader, I have found fulfillment in fostering growth and inspiration within teams. Setting collective goals and mentoring others has not only contributed to team success but has also reinforced the importance of collaboration and community—a value deeply rooted in my Kerala upbringing.

Ultimately, the practice of setting and achieving goals is a lifelong journey that continues to guide my path. By maintaining a positive mindset, embracing change, and celebrating achievements, I am empowered to pursue meaningful goals and make a lasting impact in both my career and life.

In conclusion, goal-setting is not just about defining what we want to achieve but also about fostering the mindset and habits that drive us toward success. By setting realistic goals, maintaining a positive outlook, and staying committed to our plans, we can turn our aspirations into reality and continuously grow both personally and professionally.

CHAPTER SIX

Building a Supportive Network

In the journey toward achieving personal and professional goals, having a supportive network is invaluable. A robust network provides guidance, encouragement, resources, and opportunities for collaboration. This chapter delves into the significance of building a supportive network, strategies for cultivating meaningful connections, and real-world examples from my career in the tech industry.

Community and Relationships in Positivity

Community and relationships play a pivotal role in maintaining a positive mindset, especially in a demanding field like the tech industry. The support and encouragement derived from meaningful connections can significantly influence one's mental and emotional well-being, resilience, and overall success.

Understanding the Power of Community

In a world that often feels disconnected, the power of community and relationships cannot be overstated. From my upbringing in Kalliassery, Kerala, to my professional journey in the bustling tech scene of Bangalore, I have seen firsthand how involvement in a community fosters emotional well-being and resilience. Community provides a sense of belonging and security, helping individuals navigate life's challenges with a safety net of support.

In Kerala, the sense of community is deeply ingrained in the cultural fabric. Growing up, I was immersed in a world where neighbors were more like extended family. We celebrated festivals, organized sports tournaments, and engaged in cultural activities together. These shared experiences cultivated an environment of mutual support. When I faced challenges, whether in academics or early career hurdles, the community was there, offering guidance and encouragement.

For example, during one of our village's annual football tournaments, my team faced a significant defeat. The loss was hard, but what struck me was the community's reaction. Instead of criticism, there was support and encouragement to learn from the experience. This taught me resilience and the importance of bouncing back stronger. Such shared experiences, I realized, are crucial in shaping personal growth and maintaining a positive outlook. They remind us that we are not alone, and that collective strength can propel us forward even in the toughest times.

Building Strong Relationships

Building strong relationships, whether personal or professional, is a cornerstone of maintaining a positive mindset. In Kerala, relationships are built on trust and empathy, values that I carried into my tech career in Bangalore. Trust and empathy are the foundation of any meaningful relationship. They require an investment of time and genuine interest in understanding others' perspectives and needs.

During my early days in Bangalore, adapting to a new environment while working in a high-pressure tech industry was challenging. I remember a colleague who went out of his way to help me navigate the intricacies of a complex project. His support was not just technical but also emotional. He listened to my concerns and shared his own experiences, creating an atmosphere of trust and mutual respect. This relationship was pivotal in helping me find my footing in a new city.

Effective communication is also critical in building and sustaining strong bonds. It involves not just talking but active listening and understanding. In my Kerala community, conversations often happened over shared meals or during community events, where listening was as valued as speaking. Carrying this into my professional life, I learned that taking the time to genuinely listen to colleagues and clients fosters trust and respect. It opens doors to collaboration and problem-solving, creating an environment where everyone feels valued and motivated.

Leveraging Community for Positivity

Engaging with the community and contributing to it has always been a source of positivity and personal fulfillment for me. In Kerala, community activities were a part of everyday life. Whether it was participating in Onam celebrations with intricate flower carpet competitions or volunteering during temple festivals, these activities promoted collective growth and unity. They instilled a sense of pride and belonging, fostering a positive outlook on life.

When I moved to Bangalore, I sought to recreate this sense of community by engaging in activities that allowed me to give back. Volunteering with local tech groups and participating in community service projects became a way to connect with others and contribute positively. These activities provided a break from the fast-paced tech environment and offered a different perspective on life and work.

For instance, volunteering for a tech education program for underprivileged children in Bangalore opened my eyes to the impact we can have when we come together as a community. The experience was incredibly rewarding and reminded me of the importance of giving back. It reinforced my belief that contributing to the community enhances personal fulfillment and cultivates a positive mindset.

Moreover, engaging with the community provides opportunities for learning and growth. It exposes us to diverse perspectives and ideas, encouraging us to step out of our comfort zones. In the tech industry, where innovation thrives on collaboration and diversity, leveraging community involvement can lead to new insights and breakthroughs. It reminds us that success is not just about individual achievement but about lifting each other up and moving forward together.

In conclusion, the role of community and relationships in maintaining positivity cannot be overstated. From the close-knit community in Kalliassery to the vibrant tech circles in Bangalore, I have witnessed how community involvement and strong relationships can foster resilience, support, and personal growth. By understanding the power of community, building strong relationships based on trust and empathy, and leveraging community involvement for positivity, we can create a supportive network that sustains us through life's challenges and successes. These lessons have shaped my outlook on life and work, reinforcing the belief that we are stronger together and that building a supportive network is integral to maintaining a positive and fulfilling life.

Networking in the Tech Industry: Building Meaningful Connections

The tech industry is often described as a dynamic and rapidly evolving field, where innovation and collaboration drive progress. Networking plays a pivotal role in this environment, enabling professionals to connect, collaborate, and advance their careers. For me, coming from a close-knit community in Kerala and transitioning into the bustling tech scene of Bangalore, networking has been an essential tool in building meaningful connections and fostering professional growth. Here's how I navigated this landscape and the strategies I found most effective.

Networking Strategies

Networking in the tech industry requires more than just attending events and exchanging business cards; it's about building authentic relationships that can offer mutual growth and support.

Identifying Opportunities: In the tech industry, opportunities for networking abound if you know where to look. Tech conferences, seminars, and meetups are excellent places to start. When I first moved to Bangalore, I immersed myself in the local tech scene by attending every relevant event I could find. Websites like Meetup and Eventbrite were invaluable in identifying gatherings where industry professionals came together to share insights and ideas.

Moreover, online platforms like LinkedIn offer virtual networking opportunities that transcend geographical barriers. By joining groups related to my interests and participating in discussions, I was able to connect with peers and leaders from various parts of the world. Networking doesn't always have to happen face-to-face; sometimes, the most fruitful connections are made online.

Building Rapport: Making a lasting impression and establishing genuine connections can set the foundation for a strong professional network. One of the most valuable lessons I learned from my Kerala roots is the importance of listening. In Kerala, conversations are a two-way street, where listening is as important as speaking. This skill became crucial in Bangalore, where I discovered that truly engaging with people and showing genuine interest in their work and experiences helped me build rapport.

When meeting someone new, I focused on finding common ground and asking open-ended questions that encouraged meaningful dialogue. Instead of simply exchanging pleasantries, I sought to understand their challenges, aspirations, and perspectives. This approach not only helped me make a lasting impression but also established a foundation for a genuine relationship.

Maintaining Professional Relationships

Once connections are made, maintaining those professional relationships over time requires effort and consistency. It's about nurturing the bond and ensuring it remains mutually beneficial.

Consistency and Follow-up: Staying in touch with your network is essential to maintaining strong relationships. After meeting someone at an event or through a platform, I made it a point to follow up with a personalized message, expressing my appreciation for the conversation and my interest in staying connected. This simple gesture reinforced the connection and opened the door for future interactions.

Regular check-ins are also important. Whether it's sending a quick message to congratulate someone on a recent achievement or sharing an article of mutual interest, these small actions demonstrate that you value the relationship. Consistency in communication helps keep the connection alive and shows that you are invested in maintaining the relationship over time.

Mutual Benefits: Networking is not a one-way street; it's about creating win-win scenarios where both parties benefit from the relationship. In Bangalore's tech industry, I learned that collaboration and knowledge-sharing are key to fostering reciprocal relationships. By offering my skills and insights to others, I was able to create value for them while also gaining new perspectives and opportunities.

For example, when a colleague was struggling with a project, I volunteered my expertise to help resolve the issue. This act of support strengthened our relationship and led to future collaborations where we both benefited. The key is to approach networking with a mindset of generosity and collaboration, where you seek to add value to others while also being open to receiving support.

Utilizing Networks for Career Growth

Networking is not just about building connections; it's about leveraging those relationships for personal and professional growth.

Mentorship and Guidance: One of the most significant advantages of having a robust professional network is access to mentorship and guidance. Mentors can provide invaluable insights, advice, and support, helping you navigate the complexities of your career. In Kerala, mentorship often came from community elders who shared their wisdom and experiences, guiding us through life's challenges.

In the tech industry, I sought mentors who could offer guidance on technical skills, career decisions, and personal development. By reaching out to experienced professionals within my network, I was able to gain perspectives that helped me make informed decisions and overcome obstacles. The key is to approach mentorship with humility and a willingness to learn, valuing the mentor's time and expertise.

Collaboration and Innovation: Networking can also lead to collaborative projects and innovative solutions. The diverse perspectives and expertise within a network can spark creativity and drive innovation. In Bangalore, I found that working with colleagues from different backgrounds often resulted in unique solutions to complex problems.

For instance, while working on a project aimed at improving user experience, I collaborated with a team member from a design background. Her insights into user behavior and aesthetics complemented my technical expertise, leading to a solution that was both innovative and effective. Such collaborations highlight the power of networking in bringing together diverse talents to achieve common goals.

In conclusion, networking in the tech industry is about building meaningful connections that can drive personal and professional growth. By identifying opportunities, building rapport, and maintaining relationships, we can create a supportive network that enhances our career journey. Leveraging these connections for mentorship, collaboration, and innovation further enriches our experiences and opens doors to new possibilities.

The lessons I learned from my Kerala life and tech career have shaped my approach to networking. From understanding the importance of listening and building trust to embracing collaboration and mutual benefits, these principles have guided me in creating a network that is not just a collection of contacts but a community of support and growth. As we navigate the dynamic landscape of the tech industry, let us remember that our greatest asset is our network, and by investing in it, we invest in our own success.

Stories of Support and Collaboration

During my time in Bangalore, often referred to as the Silicon Valley of India, I encountered numerous opportunities to engage in collaborative projects that emphasized the importance of teamwork, diverse perspectives, and mutual support. Coming from Kerala, where community spirit and cooperation are deeply ingrained in daily life, I found that these values played a crucial role in navigating the bustling tech scene of Bangalore. Here, I share some stories and insights from my experiences that highlight the power of support and collaboration.

Collaborative Projects and Successes

In Bangalore, collaboration was not just a buzzword but a necessity for success. The tech industry thrives on the synergy of diverse minds working together to solve complex problems and create innovative solutions.

Team Efforts: One of the most memorable projects I worked on involved developing a user-friendly app for healthcare services. Our team comprised individuals from various backgrounds—designers, developers, marketers, and healthcare professionals. Each member brought their unique expertise and perspective to the table, allowing us to create a product that was not only technically sound but also user-centric.

The success of this project was a testament to the power of teamwork. By holding regular brainstorming sessions, we fostered an environment where everyone felt comfortable sharing ideas and feedback. This open communication enabled us to identify potential challenges early and address them collaboratively. The result was an app that exceeded client expectations and improved accessibility to healthcare services for many users.

Working on this project taught me that collaboration is about leveraging the strengths of each team member. In Kerala, I had often seen community members come together to organize local festivals and events, pooling their skills and resources for a common cause. Similarly, in the tech industry, recognizing and valuing each individual's contributions is key to achieving collective success.

Innovation through Partnership: Another project that stands out involved partnering with a startup to develop an AI-driven solution for the retail industry. The collaboration between our established tech firm and the agile startup was a perfect blend of experience and fresh perspectives. While our team brought in-depth technical knowledge and industry insights, the startup team contributed innovative ideas and a willingness to experiment.

The partnership led to the creation of a cutting-edge solution that streamlined inventory management and improved customer experience. This experience highlighted how collaboration across different organizations can drive innovation. By combining resources and expertise, we were able to push the boundaries of what was possible and deliver a solution that had a significant impact on the retail sector.

In Kerala, I had witnessed how partnerships between local businesses often led to community growth and prosperity. Whether it was farmers collaborating to improve crop yields or artisans working together to market their products, the spirit of partnership was a driving force for progress. In Bangalore, I saw this principle at work on a larger scale, where collaboration between organizations could lead to industry-wide advancements.

Personal Experiences of Support

Throughout my career in Bangalore, I was fortunate to have the support of mentors, role models, and peers who played a significant role in my professional development and personal growth.

Mentors and Role Models: One of the most influential figures in my career was a senior manager who became my mentor during my early years in the tech industry. His guidance and encouragement were instrumental in helping me navigate the complexities of my role and develop the skills needed to succeed. He taught me the importance of having a clear vision and setting achievable goals, both of which have been essential in shaping my career path.

His mentorship reminded me of the community elders in Kerala who often served as guides and advisors to younger generations. Their wisdom and experience provided valuable insights that helped us make informed decisions and overcome challenges. Similarly, having a mentor in the tech industry provided me with the support and perspective needed to thrive in a competitive environment.

Peer Support: My colleagues and friends in Bangalore also played a crucial role in overcoming challenges and achieving goals. In high-pressure situations, having a supportive network of peers made all the difference. Whether it was collaborating on a challenging project or providing emotional support during difficult times, my peers were there to offer encouragement and assistance.

For example, when faced with a particularly demanding project deadline, our team pulled together to ensure its successful completion. Late nights and long hours were made bearable by the camaraderie and support we shared. This experience reinforced the importance of having a strong support network, much like the community spirit I experienced growing up in Kerala, where neighbors and friends often came together to lend a helping hand in times of need.

Lessons Learned from Collaboration

The experiences of support and collaboration in Bangalore taught me several valuable lessons about trust, cooperation, and overcoming differences.

Trust and Cooperation: Trust is the foundation of any successful collaborative endeavor. In Bangalore, I learned that trust must be earned through consistent actions and mutual respect. By being reliable and transparent in my interactions with colleagues and partners, I was able to build strong relationships based on trust.

Cooperation, too, is essential for effective collaboration. It requires open communication, active listening, and a willingness to compromise. In Kerala, cooperation was a way of life, as community members often worked together to achieve common goals. This mindset served me well in Bangalore, where cooperation was key to overcoming challenges and driving innovation.

Overcoming Differences: In a diverse team, differences in opinions and approaches are inevitable. However, these differences can be a source of strength if managed effectively. One project I worked on involved a team with diverse cultural and professional backgrounds. Initially, there were conflicts due to differing perspectives, but by fostering an environment of respect and open dialogue, we were able to turn these differences into opportunities for growth.

The key was to focus on the common goal and encourage each team member to contribute their unique insights. This experience taught me that diversity is an asset that can lead to innovative solutions and enhanced creativity. In Kerala, I had seen how diverse communities came together to celebrate festivals and events, enriching the experience with their varied traditions and customs. In Bangalore, I saw how diverse teams could achieve remarkable success by embracing their differences and working towards a shared vision.

In conclusion, my time in Bangalore was marked by numerous experiences of support and collaboration that shaped my career and personal growth. The stories of teamwork, mentorship, and peer support highlight the importance of building a supportive network in the tech industry. By embracing the values of trust, cooperation, and diversity, we can create an environment where collaboration thrives, leading to innovative solutions and collective success.

The lessons I learned from my Kerala life and tech career emphasize the power of community and collaboration. Whether in a small village or a bustling city, the principles of support and cooperation remain the same. By fostering meaningful relationships and working together towards common goals, we can achieve remarkable success and make a positive impact on the world around us.

CHAPTER SEVEN

DAILY HABITS FOR SUCCESS

Success in the tech industry, as in any field, is often the result of consistent, positive daily habits. These habits not only enhance productivity and efficiency but also contribute to maintaining a positive mindset. This chapter outlines the daily habits that have significantly contributed to my success, providing practical tips and insights for anyone seeking to achieve their goals.

Creating a Positive Daily Routine

Creating a positive daily routine is one of the most transformative practices you can adopt to enhance both your personal and professional life. By developing structured habits and rituals, you can cultivate a mindset of productivity, clarity, and peace. My journey from the tranquil village life in Kerala to the bustling tech hubs of Bangalore has taught me the value of maintaining a balanced routine, which is crucial for success and well-being.

Morning Rituals

Starting the Day Right

My mornings in Kerala were filled with the sounds of nature, setting a peaceful tone for the day. I carried this sense of tranquility into my life in Bangalore, where mornings can be quite hectic. Starting the day with a structured routine has been vital in maintaining a positive mindset. Each morning, I begin with a few minutes of meditation. This practice, rooted in ancient traditions, helps clear my mind and focus on the day ahead.

A simple ritual I learned from my grandmother was to drink a glass of warm water with lemon first thing in the morning. This not only aids in digestion but also serves as a reminder to start the day on a healthy note. As I sip my morning tea, a habit that brings back memories of Kerala's tea plantations, I review my goals for the day, ensuring that my activities align with my larger objectives.

Energizing Habits

Incorporating energizing habits into your morning routine can significantly enhance your productivity and focus. I found that even a short workout or a brisk walk can make a huge difference. During my time in Bangalore, I discovered the importance of staying active, especially when spending long hours at a desk. Engaging in physical activity, whether it's yoga or a quick jog, invigorates the body and sharpens the mind.

I also like to start the day with some reading or listening to motivational podcasts. This not only fuels my mind with new ideas but also inspires me to tackle challenges with a fresh perspective. These morning rituals set a positive tone, helping me navigate the day with enthusiasm and purpose.

Productivity Techniques

Time Management

The fast-paced tech environment in Bangalore taught me the critical importance of effective time management. Learning how to prioritize tasks and manage time efficiently has been a game-changer. One technique that has helped me tremendously is the Eisenhower Box, a decision-making tool used to prioritize tasks based on their urgency and importance.

Another strategy I employ is time-blocking, where I allocate specific time slots for different tasks throughout the day. This helps in maintaining focus and ensuring that I make progress on my goals. By setting clear boundaries around my work time, I can avoid distractions and stay on track, a practice that has proven invaluable in both personal and professional spheres.

Focus and Concentration

Enhancing focus and minimizing distractions is key to maximizing productivity. During my early days in tech, I often struggled with maintaining concentration amid various interruptions. To combat this, I developed strategies to improve focus. One of these is the Pomodoro Technique, where I work in focused bursts of 25 minutes followed by a

5-minute break. This approach helps maintain high levels of concentration and prevents burnout.

Creating a dedicated workspace is another crucial factor. In my Kerala home, a quiet corner with minimal distractions allowed me to work efficiently. I've replicated this setup in my Bangalore apartment, ensuring that my workspace is conducive to concentration and creativity.

Evening Reflection and Preparation

Winding Down: Evening routines play a vital role in relaxing the mind and preparing for the next day. Growing up in Kerala, evenings were often a time for reflection and relaxation. This habit has followed me to Bangalore, where I find it essential to unwind after a long day. Engaging in calming activities, such as reading or listening to soothing music, helps in transitioning from the day's busyness to a state of relaxation.

One practice I've found particularly helpful is writing in a journal before bed. This serves as a mental decluttering process, allowing me to unload thoughts and emotions from the day. By jotting down my experiences and reflections, I gain clarity and insight into my personal growth.

Reflective Practices: Reflection is an integral part of assessing daily achievements and identifying areas for improvement. Each evening, I review my accomplishments and challenges from the day. This practice not only helps in recognizing progress but also in understanding where I need to make adjustments.

Reflective practices are deeply rooted in my upbringing in Kerala, where introspection was often encouraged. By taking time to reflect on my actions and decisions, I've learned to cultivate a mindset of continuous improvement. This habit has been instrumental in both my personal development and professional success.

In conclusion, creating a positive daily routine is about finding balance and integrating habits that promote well-being and productivity. From the serene mornings in Kerala to the dynamic tech life in Bangalore, I have discovered that these rituals provide the foundation for success. By starting the day with intention, managing time effectively, and ending with reflection, you can cultivate a routine that supports both personal growth and professional achievement. These daily habits are not just routines; they are powerful tools that empower you to navigate life's challenges with confidence and clarity.

Incorporating Mindfulness, Gratitude, and Self-Care

Incorporating mindfulness, gratitude, and self-care into your daily life is more than just a trend; it's a vital practice for maintaining balance and well-being amidst the demands of a modern, fast-paced life. My journey from the serene village of Kalliassery in Kerala to the bustling tech environment of Bangalore has taught me the profound benefits of these practices. Here's how integrating mindfulness, cultivating gratitude, and prioritizing self-care have shaped my life and career.

Mindfulness Practices

Mindful Living

The concept of mindfulness, deeply rooted in ancient traditions, involves paying full attention to the present moment with acceptance and non-judgment. Growing up in Kerala, the slow-paced life and natural beauty encouraged a sense of calm and awareness. However, it was during my transition to the high-energy tech world in Bangalore that I realized the importance of actively incorporating mindfulness into my daily routine.

Mindfulness has been a cornerstone in managing stress and maintaining mental clarity. In the tech industry, where the pace can be relentless and the demands high, mindfulness practices have provided me with a crucial tool to stay grounded. The ability to focus on the present moment has improved my productivity and reduced anxiety, making it easier to handle the pressures of work.

Techniques and Tools

One of the most effective mindfulness techniques I've adopted is meditation. Starting with just five minutes a day, I found that this practice significantly enhanced my ability to manage stress and stay focused. Guided meditations and mindfulness apps have been particularly useful, offering structured exercises that fit into my busy schedule. These tools help in creating a moment of stillness amidst the whirlwind of daily tasks.

Another technique that has proven beneficial is mindful breathing. Simple exercises, such as taking deep, deliberate breaths while paying attention to the sensation of air entering and leaving my body, have helped me centre myself during stressful situations. This practice not only calms the mind but also sharpens focus, enhancing overall productivity.

Cultivating Gratitude

Gratitude Journaling

Expressing gratitude has been a transformative practice in my life. I began keeping a gratitude journal as a way to shift my focus from challenges to the positive aspects of my life. Each evening, I write down three things I am grateful for, no matter how small. This practice, inspired by my Kerala upbringing where appreciating simple joys was a way of life, has helped me develop a more positive outlook.

Gratitude journaling has shown me how acknowledging the good things, even amidst difficulties, can significantly boost overall well-being. It fosters a sense of contentment and helps in maintaining a balanced perspective, which is crucial in high-pressure environments like the tech industry.

Appreciating Small Moments

Recognizing and valuing small moments of joy has been another essential aspect of cultivating gratitude. During my time in Bangalore, I made it a point to appreciate the simple pleasures of daily life, whether it was savouring a cup of coffee, enjoying a quiet moment, or celebrating small victories at work. This practice has enriched my life and provided a sense of fulfilment beyond the achievements and challenges.

Incorporating these moments of appreciation into my routine has enhanced my emotional resilience. By focusing on the positives, I have been able to navigate through difficult times with greater ease and maintain a sense of balance.

Prioritizing Self-Care

Physical Well-Being

Self-care is a holistic approach to maintaining health and well-being, encompassing physical, emotional, and mental aspects. Exercise, nutrition, and rest are fundamental components of physical self-care. Growing up in Kerala, the emphasis on outdoor activities and fresh, healthy food laid the foundation for my approach to physical well-being.

In Bangalore, where the demands of a tech career can lead to a sedentary lifestyle, I have made a conscious effort to integrate exercise into my daily routine. Regular workouts, whether it's a gym session or a simple walk, have been crucial in maintaining my energy levels and overall health. Additionally, paying attention to nutrition and ensuring adequate rest have been essential in keeping up with the demands of a high-pressure environment.

Emotional Health

Nurturing emotional resilience is as important as physical health. Practices such as maintaining a positive mindset and engaging in activities that bring joy have been vital in managing stress and maintaining balance. In Kerala, the close-knit community and cultural practices provided a natural support system, and I've carried these principles into my professional life in Bangalore.

Engaging in hobbies, connecting with friends, and seeking support when needed are key practices for maintaining emotional health. I've found that dedicating time to activities I enjoy and reaching out to my support network has been invaluable in managing the emotional demands of a tech career.

Incorporating mindfulness, gratitude, and self-care into your daily routine is a powerful way to enhance well-being and maintain balance. The lessons from my Kerala upbringing and experiences in the tech industry have underscored the importance of these practices. By prioritizing mindfulness, expressing gratitude, and taking care of both physical and emotional health, you can navigate life's challenges with greater resilience and positivity. These practices are not just habits; they are essential components of a fulfilling and successful life.

Impact of Daily Habits on My Success

The integration of mindful daily habits has significantly influenced both my personal and professional success, and the journey from Kalliassery to Bangalore underscores this transformation. From the serene rhythms of village life in Kerala to the dynamic pace of the tech industry, establishing effective routines has been pivotal in shaping my growth, achievements, and overall balance.

Personal Growth and Development

Building Confidence

One of the most profound ways daily habits have contributed to my success is through the enhancement of self-esteem and personal growth. Growing up in Kalliassery, where community values and traditional practices played a significant role, I learned the importance of starting each day with purpose. This foundation laid the groundwork for the structured routines I adopted later in life.

In Bangalore's fast-paced tech environment, where the pressure to perform can be overwhelming, maintaining a positive daily routine has been essential for building and sustaining confidence. Practices like setting clear goals each day and reflecting on achievements have helped me recognize my progress and strengths. For instance, beginning my day with a mindfulness meditation has not only centered my focus but also fostered a sense of self-assurance. By taking time each morning to visualize my goals and affirm my capabilities, I've built a solid foundation of confidence that carries through to my professional endeavors.

Continuous Learning

Daily routines have also played a crucial role in fostering continuous learning and skill development. My transition from a village in Kerala to the tech industry in Bangalore required an adaptive mindset and a commitment to lifelong learning. Establishing a habit of dedicating time each day to reading industry-related articles or taking online courses has been instrumental in staying updated with technological advancements.

Incorporating learning into my daily routine has led to substantial personal growth. For example, setting aside an hour each day for self-improvement activities, such as learning new programming languages or exploring emerging technologies, has expanded my expertise and kept me competitive in the tech field. This dedication to continuous learning has not only enhanced my skill set but has also fostered a mindset of curiosity and adaptability, essential traits for navigating the ever-evolving tech landscape.

Professional Achievements

Career Success

The positive habits established through my daily routine have significantly supported my professional achievements. In the tech industry, where deadlines and high expectations are the norm, maintaining a structured approach has been critical for success. For example, using productivity techniques such as time blocking and task prioritization has enabled me to manage complex projects efficiently and meet deadlines consistently.

A specific instance highlighting the impact of these habits was a major project where tight deadlines and high stakes were involved. By adhering to a routine that included detailed planning, regular progress check-ins, and focused work sessions, I was able to lead my team to successfully deliver the project on time. This approach not only showcased the effectiveness of my daily habits but also reinforced their role in achieving professional goals.

Leadership and Influence

Consistent habits have also been pivotal in fostering effective leadership and influence. During my time in Bangalore, I realized that leading a team successfully required more than technical skills; it demanded a strong foundation of personal discipline and positive habits. By modeling a disciplined routine, including regular check-ins with team members and setting clear expectations, I was able to cultivate a productive and motivated team environment.

Additionally, my practice of mindfulness and reflection has enhanced my ability to lead with empathy and clarity. By taking time each day to reflect on my interactions and decisions, I have been able to address challenges with a balanced perspective and inspire my team to strive for excellence. This influence extends beyond individual achievements to creating a culture of support and growth within the team.

Balancing Life and Work

Harmony and Balance

Achieving a harmonious balance between personal life and professional responsibilities is a direct result of the positive daily habits I've cultivated. The structured routines I developed, such as setting clear boundaries for work hours and dedicating time to personal activities, have been instrumental in maintaining a fulfilling and balanced life.

For instance, having a consistent evening routine that includes winding down and reflecting on the day has helped me transition smoothly from work to personal time. This practice, rooted in the reflective traditions from my Kerala upbringing, ensures that I end my day with a sense of accomplishment and readiness for the next day. Balancing work with personal interests, such as continuing to participate in cultural activities and sports, has been crucial for maintaining overall well-being and avoiding burnout.

Adapting to Challenges

Daily routines have also provided a framework for navigating and overcoming life's challenges. Whether dealing with unexpected setbacks or adjusting to new circumstances, the habits I've established have offered stability and a sense of control. For example, when faced with a sudden change in project scope or personal challenges, my routine of mindfulness and goal setting has enabled me to approach these situations with resilience and adaptability.

During a particularly challenging period in my tech career, when multiple projects converged and personal responsibilities increased, adhering to my established routines proved invaluable. By sticking to my habits of setting clear priorities, maintaining regular self-care, and seeking support when needed, I was able to manage stress effectively and maintain focus. This approach not only helped me navigate the challenges but also reinforced the importance of maintaining a consistent routine to handle future obstacles.

In summary, the integration of mindfulness, gratitude, and self-care into my daily life has been instrumental in achieving personal growth, professional success, and balance. The practices that began in the tranquil setting of Kalliassery have evolved into powerful tools for navigating the complexities of the tech industry in Bangalore. By building confidence, fostering continuous learning, supporting career achievements, and maintaining harmony between work and personal life, these habits have become the cornerstone of a successful and fulfilling life

CHAPTER EIGHT

THE INTERSECTION OF TECHNOLOGY AND POSITIVITY

In the ever-evolving landscape of the digital age, technology has become an integral part of our daily lives, influencing how we think, interact, and grow. Its potential to foster a positive mindset is immense, offering tools and platforms that not only enhance mental well-being but also facilitate personal and professional growth. Drawing from my experiences in Kerala and Bangalore, I've seen firsthand how technology can be a powerful ally in nurturing positivity and resilience.

Leveraging Technology to Foster a Positive Mindset

Leveraging technology to foster a positive mindset involves utilizing digital tools and platforms to cultivate optimism, resilience, and personal growth. Here's a detailed exploration of how technology can be harnessed to promote positivity:

Digital Tools for Mindfulness and Meditation

In the hustle and bustle of modern life, finding moments of calm can be challenging. This is where digital tools for mindfulness and meditation come into play. I found apps like Headspace and Calm, which became vital in helping me manage stress and maintain mental clarity. These apps provided guided meditations, mindfulness exercises, and breathing techniques, which were especially useful during hectic workdays when taking a step back to breathe was crucial.

One particular experience stands out: after a long day of back-to-back meetings, I found myself overwhelmed and anxious. I took a break, put on my headphones, and used a guided meditation from one of these apps. Within minutes, I felt my stress levels decrease and my focus return. This small investment of time brought a significant shift in my mental state, demonstrating how accessible and effective these digital tools can be.

Beyond personal use, I encouraged my team to incorporate these practices into their routines. We began starting meetings with a short mindfulness exercise, which fostered a sense of calm and cohesion among us. This collective practice not only improved our individual well-being but also enhanced our collaboration and communication.

Online Communities and Support Networks

The power of community has always been evident to me, especially growing up in Kerala, where the sense of togetherness was woven into the fabric of daily life. In the digital realm, this sense of community is mirrored in online platforms and support networks that provide a space for connection and encouragement.

In Bangalore's tech ecosystem, I witnessed how online communities became a lifeline for many. Platforms like Reddit, LinkedIn groups, and specialized forums offered a venue for sharing knowledge, experiences, and support. When I faced challenges at work, these online spaces were invaluable for gaining new perspectives and advice from peers around the globe. They provided a reminder that I wasn't alone in my struggles and that there was a wealth of collective wisdom to tap into.

For instance, I joined an online community focused on personal development and positivity. Through engaging in discussions, sharing personal stories, and offering support to others, I experienced a profound sense of belonging and growth. These interactions not only helped me navigate professional hurdles but also inspired me to approach life with a more positive and resilient mindset.

Social media platforms also play a significant role in spreading positivity. While they can sometimes be overwhelming, when used mindfully, they can be a source of inspiration and motivation. Following accounts that focus on well-being, positivity, and personal growth filled my feed with uplifting content that encouraged me to maintain a positive outlook.

Personalized Learning and Growth

One of the most transformative aspects of technology is its ability to facilitate personalized learning and growth. In Kerala, education was always highly valued, and this ethos continued to shape my approach to learning throughout my career. Technology has made it possible to access a vast array of knowledge and skills tailored to individual needs and interests.

E-learning platforms like Coursera, Udemy, and Khan Academy have democratized education, making it accessible to anyone with an internet connection. During a pivotal point in my career, I decided to enhance my skills in data analytics, a field that was rapidly gaining importance. Through online courses, I was able to learn at my own pace, fitting study sessions around my work schedule. This flexibility allowed me to acquire new skills without disrupting my professional commitments, ultimately leading to career advancement and increased confidence.

Personalization is another key benefit of digital learning. Algorithms analyze user preferences and learning styles, curating content that resonates with individual goals. This tailored approach accelerates the learning process and ensures that the material is relevant and engaging. For me, this meant focusing on courses and content that aligned with my career aspirations, making the learning experience more meaningful and effective.

In addition to formal education, technology also supports informal learning and self-improvement. Podcasts, webinars, and virtual workshops offer opportunities to learn from experts and thought leaders, broadening horizons and sparking new ideas. By engaging with these resources, I was able to stay informed about industry trends and innovations, further fuelling my passion for growth and development.

Apps and Tools for Positivity

In today's fast-paced world, maintaining a positive outlook can be challenging. However, technology offers a plethora of apps and tools designed to support mental well-being and encourage positivity. During my journey from the serene backwaters of Kerala to the bustling tech hub of Bangalore, I've come to appreciate how these digital tools can be a valuable resource in fostering emotional health and resilience. Here's how different types of apps have contributed to maintaining a positive outlook in my life and the lives of those around me.

Mood and Emotion Tracking Apps

Mood and emotion tracking apps have become an essential tool for monitoring mental well-being. These apps allow users to record their emotional states, identify patterns, and gain insights into the factors influencing their mood. For someone like me, who has navigated the pressures of the tech industry while balancing personal life, these apps offer a window into understanding emotional fluctuations.

Monitoring Well-being: One of the most valuable aspects of these apps is their ability to track mood over time. Apps like Moodpath and Daylio allow users to log their emotions at different times of the day, providing a visual representation of emotional trends. During my career in Bangalore, I often faced the stress of meeting project deadlines and managing team dynamics. By using these apps, I could identify stress triggers and make informed decisions about managing them. For example, I noticed that my mood dipped on days with back-to-back meetings. Armed with this insight, I started scheduling short breaks to walk outside or practice deep breathing exercises, which helped improve my mood and productivity.

Data-Driven Insights: These apps also offer data-driven insights that can be incredibly revealing. They analyse the recorded data and highlight patterns, such as certain activities or times of the day that consistently affect one's mood. For instance, I discovered that my mood improved significantly on days when I engaged in physical exercise or spent time with family. This realization motivated me to incorporate regular exercise and quality family time into my routine, leading to a more balanced and positive outlook. The ability to visualize one's emotional landscape empowers individuals to take proactive steps toward enhancing their mental well-being.

Gratitude and Journaling Apps

Gratitude and journaling apps have gained popularity for their role in promoting positivity and self-reflection. These apps encourage users to cultivate gratitude and engage in reflective practices, ultimately fostering a more positive mindset.

Encouraging Gratitude: Gratitude is a powerful emotion that can transform one's perspective on life. Apps like Gratitude Journal and 5 Minute Journal make it easy to incorporate gratitude into daily routines. When I first moved to Bangalore, the fast-paced lifestyle and demands of my career left me feeling overwhelmed. However, by using these apps to jot down things I was grateful for each day, I started to focus on the positives rather than the challenges. Whether it was appreciating a colleague's support or savouring a delicious meal, these small moments of gratitude helped shift my mindset toward positivity.

Reflective Practices: Journaling apps offer a platform for self-reflection, allowing users to record their thoughts and emotions. Apps like Journey and Penzu provide a safe space to express feelings, set intentions, and track personal growth. During times of uncertainty or stress, writing down my thoughts allowed me to process my emotions and gain clarity. For instance, after a challenging day at work, I would reflect on what went well and areas for improvement. This practice helped me learn from experiences and approach similar situations with a more positive and proactive mindset.

Virtual Reality and Immersive Experiences

Virtual reality (VR) and immersive experiences have emerged as innovative tools for relaxation, stress relief, and positive visualization. These technologies transport users to different environments, offering a unique way to escape from daily stresses and cultivate a positive outlook.

Stress Reduction: VR has shown promise in reducing stress and promoting relaxation. Apps like Calm Place and Guided Meditation VR offer immersive experiences that transport users to serene landscapes or guide them through meditation sessions. When I found myself overwhelmed by work demands in Bangalore, I turned to VR for a mental escape. By putting on a VR headset and immersing myself in a tranquil forest or beach setting, I could disconnect from the chaos and recharge my mind. These experiences provided a much-needed respite, allowing me to return to work with a clearer and more positive mindset.

Positive Visualization: Immersive technology also enables users to engage in positive visualization, a technique that enhances mental well-being by imagining desired outcomes and scenarios. Apps like MindVR and Perfect Day encourage users to visualize success, happiness, and personal growth. In my tech career, where goal-setting and achievement are paramount, positive visualization has been a valuable tool. By envisioning successful project outcomes or confident presentations, I could build confidence and reduce anxiety. This practice not only boosted my performance but also reinforced a positive and optimistic mindset.

Throughout my journey from Kerala to Bangalore, I have witnessed first-hand the transformative power of technology in maintaining a positive outlook. Mood and emotion tracking apps provide valuable insights into emotional well-being, empowering individuals to make informed choices for better mental health. Gratitude and journaling apps cultivate positivity and self-reflection, while virtual reality and immersive experiences offer unique ways to reduce stress and visualize success.

By integrating these digital tools into daily life, individuals can harness the potential of technology to enhance their mental well-being and foster a positive mindset. As someone who has navigated the challenges of the tech industry and embraced the opportunities for growth, I can attest to the significant impact these tools have had on my journey. Embracing technology as an ally in maintaining positivity allows us to navigate life's ups and downs with resilience, optimism, and a greater sense of well-being.

Tech Innovations for Mental Well-Being

As the world becomes increasingly digital, technology has transformed how we approach mental well-being. From innovative apps designed to support mental health to workplace wellness programs and community-based tech initiatives, the intersection of technology and mental health is becoming more impactful than ever. Drawing from my experiences in the tech industry and personal insights from my life in Kerala and Bangalore, let's explore some compelling case studies showcasing how technology can promote mental well-being.

Successful Mental Health Apps

Innovative mental health apps have revolutionized the way individuals access mental health support. These apps provide convenient, affordable, and effective solutions for managing mental health, making it easier for people to seek help and improve their well-being.

Innovative Solutions

One of the most successful mental health apps is *Headspace*, a meditation and mindfulness platform that offers guided meditations, breathing exercises, and sleep aids. Headspace's user-friendly interface and evidence-based practices have made it a popular choice for individuals seeking to improve their mental health. Another noteworthy app is *Calm*, which focuses on meditation, relaxation, and sleep. With its soothing audio content and calming visuals, Calm has become a go-to app for stress relief and relaxation.

In Bangalore, I've seen many colleagues benefit from using these apps to manage stress and anxiety. For example, during a particularly hectic project deadline, a co-worker turned to Headspace for daily meditation sessions. These brief moments of mindfulness helped her regain focus and reduce stress, leading to a more balanced and productive work experience.

User Impact

The impact of mental health apps on individuals is profound. Consider the story of a young professional from Kerala who struggled with anxiety and insomnia. After discovering Calm, he began incorporating its guided sleep stories into his nightly routine. Over time, he noticed significant improvements in his sleep quality and overall mood. The app became a crucial part of his self-care regimen, helping him manage anxiety and enhance his well-being.

These apps empower individuals to take control of their mental health, offering accessible tools for mindfulness, relaxation, and emotional regulation. By providing support at users' fingertips, mental health apps have become valuable allies in the journey toward mental well-being.

Workplace Wellness Programs

Recognizing the importance of employee well-being, many companies are integrating technology-driven wellness programs to foster a healthy and positive work environment. These programs leverage digital tools to support employees' mental health, improve productivity, and enhance job satisfaction.

Integrating Technology

In Bangalore's fast-paced tech industry, companies like Infosys and Wipro have implemented wellness programs incorporating digital solutions. These programs often include access to mental health apps, virtual counselling services, and online wellness workshops. By leveraging technology, employers can reach a larger workforce and provide tailored support to meet individual needs.

One successful example is *Salesforce's* wellness initiative, which includes a comprehensive app that offers mindfulness exercises, virtual fitness classes, and mental health resources. This app allows employees to engage in wellness activities at their convenience, promoting a culture of self-care and well-being.

Case Studies

Consider the case of a Bangalore-based startup that partnered with a mental health app to provide employees with access to virtual therapy sessions. The app allowed employees to schedule therapy sessions with licensed therapists at their convenience, removing barriers to seeking help. This initiative not only supported employees' mental health but also resulted in increased job satisfaction and reduced burnout.

At a global tech company in Bangalore, a digital wellness platform was introduced to track employees' stress levels and provide personalized stress management techniques. The platform offered insights into individual stress triggers and suggested relaxation exercises. Employees reported feeling more supported and engaged, leading to a positive shift in the workplace culture.

These case studies highlight the power of technology in transforming workplace wellness programs. By integrating digital solutions, companies can prioritize employee well-being and create a supportive environment that fosters mental health and productivity.

Community-Based Tech Initiatives

Technology's potential to promote mental well-being extends beyond individual and workplace settings. Community-based tech initiatives leverage digital tools to create positive social impact, fostering mental health and resilience at a broader scale.

Collaborative Efforts

In Kerala, community-driven tech initiatives have emerged to address mental health challenges. One notable example is the "Mindful Kerala" project, a collaborative effort between tech professionals, mental health experts, and local organizations. The project utilizes digital platforms to provide mental health resources, online support groups, and awareness campaigns.

The initiative's success lies in its ability to connect individuals with similar experiences and provide a sense of community support. Through virtual meetups and webinars, participants can share their stories, learn coping strategies, and access professional guidance. This approach has empowered individuals to prioritize mental health and seek help when needed.

Social Impact

The impact of community-based tech initiatives is evident in the stories of individuals who have benefited from these programs. In a small village in Kerala, a digital mental health platform was introduced to support adolescents dealing with exam stress and anxiety. The platform offered interactive content, relaxation exercises, and access to mental health professionals. As a result, students reported improved stress management skills and increased academic performance.

In Bangalore, a tech-driven initiative focused on providing mental health support to underserved communities. By partnering with local NGOs and leveraging mobile technology, the initiative offered free mental health screenings, online counselling sessions, and educational resources. This effort not only raised awareness about mental health but also reduced stigma and increased access to mental health care.

These initiatives demonstrate the transformative power of technology in promoting mental well-being at a community level. By leveraging digital tools, communities can create supportive environments, reduce mental health disparities, and foster resilience.

Conclusion

In conclusion, the intersection of technology and positivity represents a powerful catalyst for personal and professional growth in today's digital age. Through innovative apps and tools, individuals can cultivate mindfulness, gratitude, and resilience, fostering a positive mindset essential for navigating challenges and achieving success.

Successful mental health apps provide individuals with accessible tools for mindfulness, relaxation, and emotional regulation. Workplace wellness programs integrate technology to support employee well-being and productivity. Community-based tech initiatives harness digital platforms to promote mental health and resilience at a broader scale.

The case studies highlight the importance of leveraging technology to foster mental well-being and create positive social impact. As a techie, I am inspired by the potential of digital tools to transform mental health care and empower individuals and communities. By embracing technology as an ally in promoting positivity, we can navigate life's challenges with resilience, optimism, and a greater sense of well-being.

Inspiring Positivity in Others

Inspiring positivity in others, particularly in professional environments, begins with leadership and setting an example that others can aspire to emulate. The ability to lead by example is essential in fostering a positive culture that can transform the dynamics of a workplace. This chapter explores how authenticity, communication, and celebration of successes contribute to creating an inspiring environment.

Inspiring Colleagues by Example

Leading by example is one of the most powerful ways to inspire positivity in your colleagues and peers. When you embody the principles you advocate, you set a standard and create a culture that others are motivated to follow. Here's how you can effectively lead by example to inspire those around you:

Embodying Positivity

Authenticity and Integrity

One of the most powerful ways to inspire positivity is to embody authenticity and integrity in all interactions. Being genuine and honest not only builds trust but also encourages others to follow suit. I recall an experience early in my career when I was working on a high-stakes project with a diverse team in Bangalore. As the project leader, I faced immense pressure to deliver results, but I realized that maintaining an open and honest communication line with my team was crucial. Instead of pretending to have all the answers, I shared my uncertainties and invited input. This openness not only made the team feel valued but also empowered them to take ownership of their roles. The project's success was a testament to the power of authentic leadership.

Emotional Intelligence

Emotional intelligence is another vital component in inspiring positivity. It involves understanding and managing your emotions and those of others. During my time in the tech industry, I often found myself in situations where high emotional intelligence was necessary. For example, during a challenging phase of product development, tensions were high, and conflicts arose frequently. By actively listening and empathizing with team members, I could diffuse tense situations and keep the team focused on common goals. Emotional awareness enabled me to motivate the team by acknowledging their feelings and channelling them toward positive outcomes. This experience underscored the importance of empathy in leadership and how it can inspire others to adopt a similar approach.

Encouraging Open Communication

Active Listening

Creating an environment where everyone feels heard and valued starts with active listening. In Kerala, where community and relationships hold significant value, I learned the importance of listening to understand rather than to respond. During my professional journey, I applied this principle by fostering an open-door policy. Team meetings were structured to ensure every member had a chance to voice their opinions. For instance, while leading a project with a cross-functional team, I noticed that some quieter team members hesitated to share their ideas. By intentionally seeking their input and acknowledging their contributions, I was able to create an inclusive environment that encouraged participation. This approach not only enhanced team morale but also led to innovative solutions that might have otherwise been overlooked.

Constructive Feedback

Providing feedback is an art that, when done right, can inspire growth and positivity. Constructive feedback involves recognizing achievements while also offering guidance for improvement. I remember working with a talented junior developer who was struggling with meeting deadlines. Instead of focusing solely on the missed targets, I highlighted the quality of his work and suggested time management strategies that could help.

This approach not only boosted his confidence but also motivated him to improve. By framing feedback as a collaborative effort toward improvement, I fostered an environment where team members felt supported and encouraged to excel.

Celebrating Success

Recognizing Achievements

Celebrating both individual and team achievements is crucial for maintaining motivation and positivity. I learned this lesson well during my early days in Kerala, where every small success was a reason for communal celebration. In the workplace, recognizing achievements reinforces positive behaviour and encourages continued effort. I recall a time when my team successfully launched a complex software update ahead of schedule. To celebrate, we organized a small gathering where everyone's contributions were acknowledged. This simple act of recognition not only boosted morale but also strengthened team cohesion. Celebrating achievements is a powerful way to show appreciation and inspire others to reach new heights.

Creating a Positive Culture

Building a workplace culture that prioritizes positivity and well-being requires deliberate effort. During my career, I discovered that culture is shaped by consistent actions and values. In Bangalore, I led initiatives that promoted a healthy work-life balance, such as flexible working hours and wellness programs. Encouraging team members to pursue personal interests and prioritizing their well-being had a profound impact on the overall atmosphere. When people feel cared for, they are more likely to contribute positively to the team and inspire others to do the same. By embedding positivity into the workplace culture, we create an environment where individuals thrive and collective success is achieved.

In Conclusion, leading by example is about embodying the values and behaviours you wish to see in others. By embracing authenticity, practicing emotional intelligence, encouraging open communication, and celebrating successes, we can inspire positivity in colleagues and peers. These actions not only enhance individual well-being but also contribute to a more harmonious and productive work environment.

Reflecting on my journey, both in Kerala and the tech world, I recognize that the principles of authenticity, empathy, and celebration have been central to inspiring positivity in others. Whether in a village community or a bustling tech hub, these principles remain timeless and universally applicable. As we strive to lead by example, we pave the way for others to do the same, creating a ripple effect of positivity that extends far beyond our immediate circles.

The Ripple Effect of Positivity in the Workplace

Creating a positive workplace culture can significantly impact an organization's success, influencing everything from collaboration to productivity. In my experiences working in Kerala and Bangalore, I've witnessed how positivity can transform team dynamics, boost morale, and improve overall performance. This section explores the various ways in which positivity creates a ripple effect throughout the workplace.

Enhancing Team Collaboration

Fostering Trust

Trust is the cornerstone of effective team collaboration, and positivity plays a crucial role in fostering it. When team members feel supported and valued, they are more likely to open up, share ideas, and work collaboratively. I remember a project in Bangalore where I was part of a diverse team tasked with developing a new software feature under tight deadlines. Initially, there was a lack of trust among team members, which hindered progress. Recognizing this, I organized team-building activities that focused on communication and understanding each other's strengths and weaknesses. By creating an environment where everyone felt comfortable sharing their thoughts and concerns, we built trust and camaraderie. This shift in dynamics enabled us to tackle challenges more effectively and deliver a successful product.

Creative Problem Solving

A positive mindset encourages innovation and creativity, essential for solving complex problems. During my career, I often noticed that teams with a positive atmosphere were more willing to take risks and explore unconventional solutions. In one instance, while working on a challenging project involving artificial intelligence, our team faced a major setback due to a technical glitch. Instead of succumbing to frustration, we approached the problem with a positive attitude, viewing it as an opportunity to learn and improve. This mindset allowed us to brainstorm creatively, leading to a breakthrough solution that not only solved the problem but also enhanced the overall functionality of our product. Positivity in the workplace fosters an environment where innovation thrives, empowering teams to push boundaries and achieve extraordinary results.

Boosting Employee Morale

Motivational Techniques

Maintaining high morale is vital for sustaining motivation and productivity. One technique I found effective in boosting morale is recognizing and celebrating individual and team achievements. Back in Kerala, community events often involved acknowledging contributions, creating a sense of belonging and motivation. I applied this principle in my professional life by implementing a "recognition board" where team members could publicly acknowledge their colleagues' efforts. This simple gesture created a culture of appreciation, motivating employees to go above and beyond in their roles. Additionally, I organized regular "fun Fridays" where the team could relax and engage in non-work-related activities, fostering a positive and enjoyable work environment. These initiatives demonstrated that motivation thrives when employees feel valued and appreciated.

Resilience Building

Positivity also plays a key role in building resilience and adaptability. In the fast-paced tech industry, challenges and setbacks are inevitable, and fostering resilience is crucial for overcoming them. I recall a project where unexpected changes in client requirements forced us to rethink our approach. Instead of viewing the situation as a failure, we embraced a positive mindset, focusing on the opportunity to learn and improve. Encouraging open discussions about challenges and framing them as learning experiences helped the team remain resilient and adaptable. This approach not only enabled us to navigate through difficulties but also strengthened our ability to handle future challenges with confidence. By cultivating positivity, we equip teams with the resilience needed to thrive in dynamic environments.

Improving Productivity and Performance

Positive Reinforcement

Positive reinforcement is a powerful tool for enhancing performance and productivity. By recognizing and rewarding desirable behaviours, organizations can create a culture of excellence. During my time in Bangalore, I led a team working on a high-stakes project that required meticulous attention to detail. To ensure high performance, I implemented a system of positive reinforcement where team members received immediate feedback and recognition for their contributions. This approach not only boosted individual confidence but also motivated the entire team to strive for excellence. As a result, we consistently met and exceeded our targets, delivering exceptional results for our clients. Positive reinforcement creates a virtuous cycle where recognition and achievement fuel motivation and productivity.

Stress Reduction

A positive work environment significantly reduces stress and enhances job satisfaction. Stress is a common challenge in the tech industry, but fostering positivity can mitigate its impact. I remember a period when our team was under immense pressure to deliver a complex project. By prioritizing open communication, we created a supportive environment where team members felt comfortable expressing their concerns and seeking help. Additionally, I encouraged regular breaks and mindfulness practices to promote well-being. This focus on positivity and well-being helped reduce stress levels, allowing the team to remain focused and motivated. Ultimately, a positive work environment enhances employee satisfaction and performance, contributing to the organization's overall success.

In conclusion, the ripple effect of positivity in the workplace extends beyond individual interactions, influencing team dynamics, morale, and productivity. By fostering trust and creativity, we enhance collaboration and innovation. Boosting morale through recognition and motivational techniques creates a culture of appreciation, while resilience building equips teams to navigate challenges with confidence. Positive reinforcement enhances performance, and a supportive environment reduces stress, promoting job satisfaction.

Reflecting on my experiences in Kerala and Bangalore, I recognize that the principles of positivity are universal and timeless. Whether in a small village or a bustling tech hub, positivity has the power to transform workplaces and drive success. By embracing positivity, we create environments where individuals and teams can thrive, fostering a culture of excellence and well-being.

Mentorship and Its Impact on Professional Growth

Mentorship is a crucial component in the development of professional skills and career advancement. A mentor provides guidance, support, and feedback, helping mentees navigate their career paths more effectively. The impact of mentorship on professional growth is multifaceted, influencing everything from technical skills to personal development and leadership abilities. Here, we will delve into the various aspects of mentorship and how it can significantly enhance professional growth.

Building Meaningful Mentor-Mentee Relationships

Finding the Right Mentor

Identifying the right mentor is a pivotal step in a successful mentorship journey. During my early years in Kerala, I was fortunate to have a mentor who not only shared his technical expertise but also encouraged me to think creatively and embrace challenges. Finding the right mentor is not just about seeking someone with the right skills; it's about connecting with an individual whose values and vision align with yours. Look for someone who inspires you, challenges your assumptions, and encourages you to explore new horizons.

In Bangalore, where the tech industry thrives on innovation, I had the opportunity to connect with several mentors who provided invaluable guidance. When seeking a mentor, attend industry events, engage in professional networks, and don't hesitate to reach out to potential mentors with whom you resonate. A well-chosen mentor can provide the insights and perspectives needed to navigate the complexities of your career.

Mutual Learning

Mentorship is a two-way street where both the mentor and mentee have opportunities to learn and grow. While my mentors have imparted invaluable wisdom, I have also been able to share fresh perspectives and ideas with them. This mutual exchange fosters a dynamic relationship where both parties benefit. In my role as a mentor, I have found that mentees often bring innovative ideas and approaches that challenge my thinking, leading to a richer learning experience for both of us.

During a project in Bangalore, one of my mentees introduced me to a new coding methodology that revolutionized our approach. This experience underscored the importance of being open to learning from those you mentor. Encourage an environment where open dialogue and knowledge sharing are prioritized, as this not only enriches the relationship but also drives innovation and growth.

Mentorship in Action

Sharing Knowledge

Effective mentorship involves more than imparting knowledge; it's about inspiring growth and encouraging exploration. I recall a pivotal moment when one of my mentors in Kerala challenged me to lead a project that was beyond my comfort zone. This challenge pushed me to apply theoretical knowledge in a practical setting, significantly boosting my confidence and skills.

As a mentor, sharing knowledge involves guiding mentees through real-world challenges, offering feedback, and encouraging them to think critically. Encourage mentees to explore their interests, provide resources for further learning, and share personal experiences that offer insights into the industry's nuances. By being approachable and available, you create a supportive environment where mentees feel empowered to ask questions and seek guidance.

Goal Setting and Accountability

A key aspect of mentorship is helping mentees set and achieve meaningful goals. When I first started my career in Bangalore, a mentor helped me outline clear, achievable goals that aligned with my aspirations. This clarity enabled me to focus my efforts and track my progress effectively. As a mentor, assist your mentees in setting SMART (Specific, Measurable, Achievable, Relevant, Time-bound) goals that align with their career objectives.

Moreover, hold mentees accountable for their goals by regularly reviewing their progress and providing constructive feedback. Encourage them to celebrate small victories and learn from setbacks. By fostering a goal-oriented mindset, you equip your mentees with the tools they need to succeed in their careers.

Long-Term Impact of Mentorship

Career Advancement

Mentorship plays a crucial role in career advancement, offering guidance and support as individuals navigate their professional journeys. Throughout my career, mentors have provided me with the insights and confidence needed to pursue opportunities I might have otherwise overlooked. In Bangalore, a mentor once recommended me for a leadership position, a role that significantly shaped my career trajectory.

Mentors provide not only guidance but also advocacy, helping mentees access new opportunities and networks. Encourage your mentees to take calculated risks, explore diverse roles, and continuously seek ways to grow professionally. By instilling confidence and offering strategic advice, you help pave the way for their career advancement.

Cultivating Future Leaders

The true impact of mentorship lies in its ability to inspire the next generation of leaders. By fostering a culture of mentorship, organizations can cultivate a pipeline of skilled, confident, and innovative leaders. Reflecting on my experiences in Kerala, I am reminded of how community elders mentored young individuals, instilling values of integrity and leadership that transcended professional settings.

As a mentor, focus on developing not just technical skills but also leadership qualities such as empathy, resilience, and adaptability. Encourage mentees to embrace leadership opportunities, support their development as they navigate challenges, and empower them to lead with authenticity and integrity. By inspiring future leaders, you contribute to creating a positive and enduring legacy within your organization and industry.

Mentorship is a powerful catalyst for professional growth, fostering meaningful relationships, facilitating knowledge sharing, and inspiring future leaders. By finding the right mentor, engaging in mutual learning, and applying mentorship in action, individuals can unlock their full potential and achieve remarkable success.

Reflecting on my experiences in Kerala and Bangalore, I am reminded of the profound impact that mentorship has had on my career. Whether through guidance, advocacy, or inspiration, mentors have been instrumental in shaping my path and empowering me to make a positive impact. As you embark on your mentorship journey, remember that the ripple effects of mentorship extend far beyond individual achievements, influencing organizations, industries, and communities.

In closing, I encourage you to seek out mentorship opportunities, both as a mentee and a mentor. Embrace the transformative power of mentorship and its ability to inspire positivity, growth, and innovation. By investing in meaningful mentor-mentee relationships, we contribute to a brighter, more connected, and prosperous future for all.

Conclusion

Inspiring positivity in others is a powerful way to create a supportive and thriving work environment. Leading by example, demonstrating a positive attitude, and fostering open communication are crucial steps in setting the tone for a culture of positivity. When leaders show respect, empathy, and integrity, they build trust and motivate their teams to achieve collective goals.

The ripple effect of positivity extends beyond individual interactions, enhancing team dynamics, boosting morale, and promoting overall well-being. By encouraging personal and professional development, fostering collaboration, and recognizing achievements, leaders can create a workplace where everyone feels valued and motivated.

Mentorship plays a vital role in this process, offering guidance, support, and opportunities for growth. As mentors, we can inspire the next generation of leaders, helping them navigate their career paths and overcome challenges with confidence and resilience.

Ultimately, the impact of inspiring positivity in others is profound. It leads to a more cohesive, productive, and innovative work environment, where individuals are empowered to reach their full potential. By cultivating a positive mindset and leading with empathy and integrity, we can make a lasting difference in the lives of our colleagues and contribute to the success of our organizations.

CHAPTER TEN

SUSTAINING POSITIVITY FOR THE LONG TERM

Maintaining a positive mindset over the long term is essential for sustained personal and professional success. This chapter explores strategies and practices that contribute to lasting positivity, enabling individuals to navigate challenges, maintain motivation, and cultivate a fulfilling life.

Strategies for Sustaining Positivity

Establishing Healthy Habits

In my early career as a techie in Bangalore, I quickly learned that establishing healthy habits was key to maintaining a positive mindset amidst the rapid pace and demands of the industry. The importance of consistency and routine cannot be overstated. A structured daily routine not only helps streamline your tasks but also ensures that you are making time for activities that nurture your well-being.

Starting my day with a morning routine sets a positive tone for the rest of the day. I found that incorporating a few minutes of meditation and stretching helps clear my mind and energize my body. These practices allow me to approach the day's challenges with a calm and focused mindset. The simple act of taking deep breaths and visualizing a productive day ahead can have a profound impact on my mood and motivation.

Another crucial aspect of establishing healthy habits is recognizing the mind-body connection. As a tech professional, I often found myself sitting for long hours, which could easily lead to physical and mental fatigue. To counter this, I made it a priority to integrate physical activity into my routine. Whether it's a brisk walk around the block or a quick workout session, these activities boost my energy levels and enhance my mental clarity.

Additionally, maintaining a balanced diet plays a vital role in supporting a positive mindset. In Kerala, where I grew up, the emphasis on fresh, wholesome foods instilled in me the value of nourishing my body with the right nutrients. Incorporating fruits, vegetables, and whole grains into my diet helps me sustain energy throughout the day and keeps my mood stable.

Cultivating Positive Relationships

Building and nurturing positive relationships has been a cornerstone of sustaining long-term positivity in both my personal and professional life. In Kerala, the sense of community is strong, and this has greatly influenced my approach to relationships. Surrounding yourself with positive and encouraging individuals creates an environment where you feel supported and uplifted.

Throughout my career in Bangalore, I have been fortunate to meet individuals who inspire and motivate me. Building a supportive network requires a conscious effort to connect with people who share similar values and goals. Engaging in meaningful conversations and actively listening to others fosters a sense of empathy and understanding, which strengthens relationships.

Empathy plays a significant role in sustaining healthy relationships and a positive mindset. By putting ourselves in others' shoes and truly understanding their perspectives, we create a space for open communication and mutual respect. In my tech career, I often collaborated with diverse teams, and practicing empathy allowed me to navigate differences and find common ground.

Compassion is another essential element in cultivating positive relationships. Showing kindness and understanding toward others creates a ripple effect of positivity. When colleagues face challenges or setbacks, offering a helping hand or words of encouragement can make a significant difference in their outlook. This compassionate approach fosters an environment where individuals feel valued and motivated to contribute their best.

Fostering Resilience and Adaptability

Resilience and adaptability are vital qualities for sustaining positivity, especially in the fast-paced world of technology. In my journey from Kerala to Bangalore, I encountered various challenges that required me to embrace change and adapt to new circumstances. These experiences taught me valuable lessons in resilience and positivity.

Embracing change is not always easy, but it is essential for personal and professional growth. I have learned that viewing change as an opportunity for learning and development rather than a source of stress is a powerful mindset shift. This perspective allows me to remain open to new experiences and approaches.

One technique that has been instrumental in maintaining positivity through change is focusing on what I can control. In the ever-evolving tech industry, external factors may be beyond my influence, but I can choose how I respond to them. By setting realistic goals and maintaining a positive attitude, I can navigate change with confidence and determination.

Learning from challenges is another crucial aspect of fostering resilience. Each obstacle presents an opportunity for growth and self-improvement. Reflecting on past experiences and extracting lessons from them enables me to approach future challenges with greater wisdom and resilience.

During my time in Bangalore, I faced setbacks that initially seemed insurmountable. However, I discovered that embracing a growth mindset allowed me to view these challenges as stepping stones toward success. For example, when a project did not go as planned, instead of dwelling on the failure, I focused on identifying areas for improvement and implementing changes to achieve better outcomes in the future.

Ultimately, fostering resilience and adaptability requires a commitment to personal growth and a willingness to step outside of one's comfort zone. It involves embracing change with an open mind and a positive outlook, knowing that each experience contributes to your development and strengthens your ability to thrive in any situation.

In conclusion, sustaining positivity for the long term requires a multifaceted approach that encompasses healthy habits, positive relationships, and resilience. By establishing consistent routines that prioritize physical and mental well-being, we can lay the foundation for a positive mindset. Cultivating positive relationships through empathy and compassion enriches our lives and creates a supportive environment for personal and professional growth.

Furthermore, fostering resilience and adaptability equips us to navigate challenges with confidence and embrace change as an opportunity for learning. The journey from Kerala to Bangalore has taught me that sustaining positivity is not a destination but an ongoing process. It is about continuously nurturing the habits and mindset that empower us to thrive and inspire others along the way. As we strive to maintain a positive outlook, let us remember that every small step we take contributes to a brighter and more fulfilling future.

Handling Setbacks and Staying Motivated

Navigating setbacks and maintaining motivation can be one of the most challenging aspects of personal and professional life. Drawing from my experiences in tech and personal life in Kerala, where resilience was often required, I've learned a lot about how to keep moving forward even when the going gets tough.

Emotional Regulation

Understanding and managing emotions is crucial when dealing with setbacks. In the tech industry, where rapid changes and high expectations are common, it's easy to become overwhelmed. I remember a time early in my career when a major project failure left me feeling disheartened. The pressure was immense, and the initial reaction was frustration and doubt. But it was during this time that I learned the importance of emotional regulation.

One technique that proved invaluable was **mindfulness**. Practicing mindfulness helps in recognizing and accepting emotions without letting them control your actions. It's about taking a step back and observing your feelings objectively. For instance, I started incorporating short mindfulness sessions into my daily routine. These sessions weren't about eliminating stress but about understanding and managing it. I would spend a few minutes each day simply observing my thoughts and feelings, which helped me gain perspective and avoid being consumed by negativity.

Stress managementtools also played a significant role. Techniques such as deep breathing exercises and progressive muscle relaxation became part of my toolkit. Whenever a stressful situation arose, I would take a moment to practice these techniques. It wasn't about erasing stress but about creating a buffer that allowed me to approach challenges with a clearer mind. Over time, this practice became second nature, helping me to stay calm and focused, even during high-pressure situations.

Developing a Growth Mindset

Adopting a growth mindset is another critical element in overcoming setbacks. Embracing challenges as opportunities for learning rather than obstacles to avoid can transform how you approach difficulties. In the tech world, where innovation often comes with failure, this mindset is particularly relevant.

I recall a project where our team faced a significant setback due to unforeseen technical issues. It was tempting to view the situation as a failure, but instead, we chose to see it as a learning opportunity. We conducted a thorough post-mortem analysis, identifying what went wrong and how we could improve. This shift in perspective turned a disappointing outcome into a valuable learning experience. It was this approach that not only helped us recover but also improved our processes and performance in future projects.

Setting realistic goals is another crucial aspect of maintaining motivation. After experiencing setbacks, it's easy to set overly ambitious goals in an attempt to make up for lost ground. However, setting achievable and incremental goals is more effective. For example, after a significant project failure, I focused on setting smaller, manageable objectives that aligned with long-term goals. This approach not only kept me motivated but also provided a sense of accomplishment as I met each milestone.

Seeking Support and Guidance

No one navigates setbacks alone, and seeking support is a crucial step in maintaining motivation. During my early career, I found that reaching out for help was a sign of strength, not weakness. Finding mentors and peers who could offer advice, encouragement, and perspective was incredibly beneficial.

I recall a particularly challenging period when I was struggling with balancing work and personal life. I reached out to a mentor who had navigated similar challenges. Their guidance was invaluable, providing practical advice on time management and stress reduction. This support not only helped me through that difficult time but also reinforced the importance of building a network of trusted advisors.

Utilizing resources effectively also involves seeking professional help when needed. There were times when talking to a career coach or counselor provided a fresh perspective and actionable strategies for overcoming obstacles. Professional guidance can offer new insights and techniques that might not be apparent from within the situation. For example, during a period of intense stress, I sought out a career counselor who helped me develop strategies for managing work pressure and maintaining a positive outlook.

In summary, dealing with setbacks and staying motivated involves a combination of emotional regulation, developing a growth mindset, and seeking support. By incorporating mindfulness practices, embracing challenges as learning opportunities, setting realistic goals, and leveraging support networks, we can navigate setbacks more effectively and maintain our motivation. These strategies have been instrumental in my journey through both the tech world and personal life in Kerala, offering practical tools and insights for sustaining positivity over the long term.

Personal Growth and Continuous Learning

Personal growth and continuous learning have been vital elements of my journey, both in my career and personal life. Reflecting on my experiences, from my tech career in Bangalore to my roots in Kerala, I've seen how an attitude of curiosity, self-reflection, and goal-setting can significantly shape one's path.

Lifelong Learning

Curiosity and Exploration

Growing up in Kerala, I was always surrounded by nature, culture, and stories that sparked my curiosity. I remember spending hours by the village pond, pondering the simple yet profound workings of life around me. This innate curiosity never left me, and it became a driving force as I transitioned into the tech industry. In a field that is constantly evolving, the willingness to explore new ideas and technologies is essential. It's this sense of curiosity that pushes you to ask questions, seek out new information, and continuously evolve.

In my early career, I found myself working on projects that were outside my comfort zone. Instead of shying away, I embraced these opportunities as a chance to learn. I dived into unfamiliar software and tools, not just because they were necessary for the job, but because they intrigued me. This mindset of exploration helped me build a diverse skill set, which became a strong foundation for my career growth.

Cultivating curiosity isn't just about professional development; it's a way of life. Whether it's picking up a new hobby, reading a book outside your usual genre, or traveling to a place you've never been, these experiences broaden your perspective and enrich your life. Curiosity fuels personal growth by opening doors to new experiences and learning opportunities that you might not have considered otherwise.

Learning Opportunities

Identifying and pursuing learning opportunities has been crucial in both my professional and personal development. In the tech industry, continuous learning isn't just encouraged—it's required. I've always been on the lookout for courses, workshops, and seminars that could add to my knowledge and skills. For example, when I noticed the growing importance of data science in our projects, I enrolled in an online course to learn the basics. This proactive approach not only equipped me with new skills but also made me more valuable to my team and opened up new career opportunities.

Outside of formal education, learning opportunities are everywhere. One of the most impactful lessons I've learned is that growth often happens in the unlikeliest of places. A casual conversation with a colleague, a challenging project, or even a failure can be a powerful learning experience. For instance, a project I was working on in Bangalore once faced a critical issue just before the deadline. It was a stressful situation, but it forced me to think creatively and work under pressure. The lessons I learned from that experience—problem-solving, resilience, and teamwork—were far more valuable than any formal training could provide.

Personal growth is not limited to career advancement. Learning opportunities in life, such as taking up a new hobby or volunteering, contribute to overall well-being and happiness. In Kerala, I've always been involved in community activities, which taught me a lot about leadership, empathy, and the importance of giving back. These experiences, though not directly related to my profession, have played a significant role in shaping my character and values.

Reflective Practices

Self-Reflection

Self-reflection is a practice that has guided me through many phases of growth. It's about taking the time to pause, think, and assess where you are and where you want to go. In my tech career, I've often found that regular self-reflection helps me stay aligned with my goals. After completing a project, I would take a step back and reflect on what went well, what didn't, and what I could do better next time. This practice allowed me to continuously improve and avoid repeating mistakes.

Self-reflection isn't just about looking at the past; it's also about envisioning the future. In Kerala, where life moves at a slower pace, I found it easier to engage in this practice. Whether it was during a quiet evening walk through the village or while sitting by the river, these moments of solitude provided the perfect backdrop for introspection. Reflecting on my values, aspirations, and the lessons learned along the way helped me stay grounded and focused.

Incorporating self-reflection into your daily routine can be as simple as journaling for a few minutes each day or setting aside time to meditate. The key is consistency. Over time, these small acts of reflection accumulate, leading to greater self-awareness and growth. It's a practice that not only helps in making better decisions but also in appreciating the journey of life.

Feedback and Growth

Feedback is a powerful tool for personal and professional growth, but it's often underutilized. In the early days of my career, I was hesitant to seek feedback, fearing criticism. However, I soon realized that constructive feedback is essential for improvement. I began actively seeking feedback from colleagues and mentors, not just when things went wrong, but also when they went right. This practice of soliciting feedback allowed me to identify blind spots, refine my skills, and grow as a professional.

One of the most impactful pieces of feedback I received was during a project in Bangalore. My mentor pointed out that while I was technically proficient, I needed to work on my communication skills to effectively lead a team. This feedback, though initially hard to accept, became a turning point. I took it to heart and began focusing on improving my communication, which eventually led to better team dynamics and more successful project outcomes.

Feedback isn't limited to the workplace. In personal life, feedback from friends, family, or community members can provide valuable insights into our behavior and its impact on others. For example, after organizing a community event in Kerala, I sought feedback from participants to understand what worked well and what could be improved. This not only helped in planning better events in the future but also strengthened my relationships with the community.

Goal Setting and Achievement

Vision and Planning

Setting goals has always been a central part of my growth strategy. Whether in my tech career or personal life, having a clear vision and a plan to achieve it has kept me motivated and on track. I remember when I first moved to Bangalore; I set a goal to learn as much as possible about the latest technologies and advance in my career. I broke this goal down into smaller, manageable steps, such as taking specific courses, attending industry conferences, and seeking mentorship. This approach made the larger goal less daunting and more achievable.

Goal setting isn't just about professional achievements. Personal goals are equally important for overall happiness and fulfillment. For instance, one of my personal goals was to maintain a strong connection with my roots in Kerala despite living in a bustling city like Bangalore. I made it a point to visit my village regularly, stay involved in community activities, and preserve the traditions and values that shaped me. This goal kept me grounded and provided a sense of balance in my life.

Celebrating Milestones

Recognizing and celebrating milestones is essential for maintaining motivation and positivity. In the fast-paced tech world, it's easy to move from one project to the next without taking the time to appreciate what's been accomplished. However, I've learned that celebrating successes, no matter how small, is crucial for staying motivated. After completing a challenging project, I would often take my team out for a celebratory meal or organize a small event to acknowledge everyone's hard work. These moments of celebration not only boosted morale but also reinforced the importance of teamwork and perseverance.

In personal life, celebrating milestones is equally important. Whether it's a birthday, a wedding anniversary, or achieving a personal goal, these celebrations provide a sense of accomplishment and joy. I've always cherished the traditions in Kerala, where even the simplest of achievements are celebrated with enthusiasm. These celebrations create lasting memories and strengthen bonds with loved ones.

In conclusion, personal growth and continuous learning are ongoing processes that require curiosity, self-reflection, goal setting, and the celebration of achievements. By embracing these practices, we can navigate the complexities of life with a positive mindset and a sense of purpose. My journey, from the tranquil landscapes of Kerala to the dynamic tech industry in Bangalore, has been shaped by these principles, and they continue to guide me as I strive for growth and fulfillment.

Conclusion: Embracing the Journey

Throughout this book, we've explored the transformative power of positivity and its profound impact on personal and professional success. From understanding the nuances of a positive mindset to navigating setbacks, fostering resilience, and sustaining optimism, each chapter has been a testament to the journey of growth and self-discovery.

Recap of Key Points and Lessons Learned

1. Understanding Positivity:

- Positivity is more than just a state of mind; it's a mindset that influences how we perceive and respond to the world around us.
- Cultivating positivity involves practices such as mindfulness, gratitude, and positive affirmations, which help us maintain emotional balance and resilience.

2. Navigating Setbacks:

- Setbacks are inevitable in life and career. They provide opportunities for growth and learning.
- Strategies for dealing with setbacks include acknowledging emotions, reframing negative thoughts, seeking support, and staying persistent in pursuit of goals.

3. Personal Growth and Continuous Learning:

- Personal growth is a lifelong journey of self-improvement and development.
- Continuous learning through formal education, informal experiences, and seeking feedback enhances adaptability, innovation, and personal fulfillment.

4. Building Resilient Relationships:

- Supportive relationships play a crucial role in maintaining positivity and emotional well-being.
- Building trust, empathy, and open communication fosters strong connections that provide encouragement, advice, and a sense of community.

5. Goal Setting and Achievement:

- Setting clear, achievable goals provides direction and motivation for personal and professional growth.
- Celebrating small wins and staying committed to long-term objectives reinforces positivity and boosts self-confidence.

6. Embracing Change and Adaptability:

- Positivity enables us to embrace change with resilience and adaptability.
- Viewing challenges as opportunities for growth and innovation fosters a proactive approach to navigating uncertainty and achieving success.

7. Practicing Self-Compassion and Wellness:

- Self-care, including physical health, mental well-being, and managing stress, is essential for sustaining positivity.
- Practicing self-compassion and nurturing a positive self-image enhances resilience and emotional strength during difficult times.

8. Leveraging Technology and Innovation:

- Technology can be harnessed to foster positivity through tools for mindfulness, productivity, and maintaining social connections.
- Innovations promoting mental well-being highlight the intersection of technology and personal growth in today's digital age.

9. Inspiring and Supporting Others:

- Leading by example and nurturing a positive environment inspires colleagues and peers to adopt similar mindsets.
- The ripple effect of positivity in the workplace enhances teamwork, morale, and collective success.

10. Sustaining Positivity for the Long Term:

- Sustaining positivity requires ongoing commitment to personal growth, resilience, and maintaining supportive networks.
- Embracing the journey of self-discovery and continuous improvement leads to a fulfilling and purposeful life.

Lessons Learned

- **Positivity is a Choice:** Cultivating a positive mindset involves intentional practices and a commitment to self-reflection and personal growth.
- **Resilience Builds Strength:** Embracing challenges and setbacks as opportunities for learning and growth enhances resilience and emotional fortitude.
- **Support Networks Matter:** Building and nurturing supportive relationships provides encouragement, guidance, and perspective during times of uncertainty.
- **Continuous Learning Fuels Growth:** Lifelong learning fosters adaptability, innovation, and a proactive approach to personal and professional development.
- **Self-Care is Essential:** Prioritizing self-care and well-being sustains positivity and strengthens our capacity to navigate life's ups and downs.

Embracing a Positive Mindset

Embracing a positive mindset across all aspects of life is not just beneficial but essential for personal well-being, growth, and success. Here's a detailed exploration of why and how to encourage this mindset:

Importance of Embracing a Positive Mindset

1. **Enhanced Resilience and Adaptability:**

   - A positive mindset strengthens resilience, helping individuals bounce back from setbacks and adapt to changes effectively. It allows for a more flexible and proactive approach to life's challenges.

2. **Improved Mental and Emotional Well-being:**

○ Positivity fosters emotional balance, reducing stress and anxiety levels. It promotes a healthier perspective on setbacks and encourages a more optimistic outlook on life.

3. **Increased Motivation and Productivity:**

○ When individuals maintain a positive mindset, they are more motivated to pursue goals and take proactive steps towards personal and professional achievements. This positivity fuels productivity and fosters a proactive attitude.

4. **Stronger Relationships and Support Networks:**

○ Positive individuals tend to build stronger, more supportive relationships. They inspire trust, empathy, and collaboration, which are essential for personal growth and a fulfilling social life.

5. **Enhanced Problem-Solving Skills:**

○ Optimistic thinking enhances cognitive flexibility and creativity, enabling individuals to approach problems with innovative solutions. It encourages a growth mindset, where challenges are viewed as opportunities for learning and improvement.

Strategies to Embrace a Positive Mindset

1. **Practice Gratitude and Mindfulness:**

○ Cultivate gratitude by acknowledging and appreciating the positive aspects of life, no matter how small. Practice mindfulness to stay present and focused on the present moment, reducing worry about the future or regret about the past.

2. Challenge Negative Thoughts:

- Identify and challenge negative thoughts or self-doubt. Replace them with positive affirmations and realistic perspectives. This shift in mindset can significantly improve overall outlook and resilience.

3. Set Meaningful Goals:

- Establish clear, achievable goals that align with personal values and aspirations. Break down larger goals into smaller, manageable steps, celebrating milestones along the way. Goal achievement reinforces positivity and boosts self-confidence.

4. Surround Yourself with Positivity:

- Surround yourself with supportive, optimistic people who uplift and encourage you. Limit exposure to negativity and cultivate environments—both physical and virtual—that promote positivity and personal growth.

5. Practice Self-Care:

- Prioritize self-care activities that promote physical, mental, and emotional well-being. This includes regular exercise, adequate sleep, healthy eating habits, and engaging in hobbies or activities that bring joy and relaxation.

6. Learn from Setbacks and Challenges:

- View setbacks and challenges as opportunities for growth and learning. Reflect on experiences, identify lessons learned, and consider how you can adapt and improve in similar situations in the future. This mindset shifts fosters resilience and continuous improvement.

Encouragement to Embrace Positivity

Embracing a positive mindset is a journey that requires commitment and practice. Encourage yourself and others to approach life with optimism, resilience, and a proactive attitude. Celebrate successes, learn from failures, and support each other in cultivating a mindset that fosters personal growth and fulfillment.

By integrating these strategies into daily life, individuals can create a foundation for sustained positivity and resilience across all aspects of life. Embracing a positive mindset not only enhances personal well-being but also contributes to a more compassionate and supportive community, where individuals thrive and inspire others to do the same.

Final Thoughts and a Call to Action

As we conclude this exploration of positivity and personal growth, it's essential to reflect on the transformative power of a positive mindset and its profound impact on our lives. Throughout this journey, we've uncovered strategies to cultivate resilience, enhance well-being, and foster meaningful connections. Now, let's distil these insights into actionable steps to empower ourselves and others:

Embrace Positivity as a Lifestyle

1. **Mindset Matters:** Recognize that positivity is not just a fleeting emotion but a conscious choice to approach life with optimism and resilience. Cultivate gratitude, practice mindfulness, and challenge

negative thoughts to nurture a positive mindset daily.

2. **Set Inspiring Goals:** Define clear, achievable goals that align with your values and aspirations. Break them down into actionable steps, celebrate milestones, and stay committed to continuous growth and improvement.

3. **Build Supportive Networks:** Surround yourself with supportive, optimistic individuals who uplift and encourage you. Foster authentic connections, offer support, and seek guidance from mentors who inspire and guide your journey.

4. **Embrace Challenges:** View challenges as opportunities for growth and learning. Embrace discomfort, step out of your comfort zone, and approach setbacks with resilience and determination. Each obstacle overcome strengthens your character and resilience.

5. **Practice Self-Care:** Prioritize self-care to nurture your physical, mental, and emotional well-being. Establish healthy habits, maintain a balanced lifestyle, and engage in activities that replenish your energy and bring joy.

Call to Action: Inspire and Empower

1. **Share Your Journey:** Share your experiences, insights, and lessons learned with others. By sharing your journey of personal growth and positivity, you inspire and empower those around you to embark on their own paths of self-discovery and resilience.

2. **Support Others:** Offer encouragement, lend a listening ear, and celebrate the successes of those in your community. Supportive relationships and acts of kindness create ripple effects of positivity and contribute to a thriving, compassionate environment.

3. **Commit to Continuous Learning:** Stay curious, seek new knowledge, and embrace lifelong learning. Stay abreast of developments in your field, explore new interests, and challenge yourself to grow intellectually and professionally.

4. **Practice Gratitude:** Cultivate a habit of gratitude by acknowledging and appreciating the blessings in your life, both big and small. Gratitude fosters resilience, enhances well-being, and nurtures a positive outlook on life.
5. **Take Action:** Commit to taking proactive steps towards your goals and aspirations. Whether it's pursuing a passion project, advancing your career, or making a positive impact in your community, every action you take contributes to your personal growth and the collective well-being of those around you.

By integrating these principles into your daily life and encouraging others to do the same, you contribute to a world where optimism, kindness, and growth thrive. Together, let's continue to cultivate positivity, inspire meaningful change, and empower each other to live purposefully and joyfully.

Appendix

Recommended Books, Apps, and Websites

In this section, we provide a detailed list of recommended books, apps, and websites to support your journey toward cultivating positivity, personal growth, and resilience. These resources span various categories, including mindfulness, goal-setting, self-care, and professional development.

Recommended Books

1. **"The Power of Now" by Eckhart Tolle**

   - **Summary:** This book emphasizes the importance of living in the present moment and letting go of past regrets and future anxieties.
   - **Why Read It:** It provides practical advice and spiritual insights for achieving a state of mindfulness and inner peace.

2. **"Atomic Habits" by James Clear**

   - **Summary:** James Clear explains how small, incremental habits can lead to significant improvements in life and productivity.
   - **Why Read It:** It offers actionable strategies for building good habits and breaking bad ones, backed by scientific research.

3. **"Grit: The Power of Passion and Perseverance" by Angela Duckworth**

   - **Summary:** Angela Duckworth explores the importance of grit—passion and perseverance—in achieving long-term goals.
   - **Why Read It:** It provides insights into how resilience and sustained effort contribute to success more than talent alone.

4. **"Mindset: The New Psychology of Success" by Carol S. Dweck**

- **Summary:** Carol Dweck discusses the concept of fixed and growth mindsets and how they influence success and personal development.
- **Why Read It:** It helps readers understand how their mindset shapes their approach to challenges and learning.

5. "The Happiness Advantage" by Shawn Achor

- **Summary:** This book explores the relationship between positivity and success, presenting research-backed strategies for boosting happiness.
- **Why Read It:** It demonstrates how a positive mindset can improve performance and well-being in various aspects of life.

6. "Daring Greatly" by Brené Brown

- **Summary:** Brené Brown discusses the power of vulnerability and how embracing it can lead to a more fulfilling life.
- **Why Read It:** It encourages readers to be courageous, embrace their vulnerabilities, and foster deeper connections with others.

7. "The 7 Habits of Highly Effective People" by Stephen R. Covey

- **Summary:** This classic book outlines seven habits that can lead to personal and professional effectiveness.
- **Why Read It:** It provides timeless principles for achieving goals and improving productivity.

Recommended Apps

1. Headspace

- **Purpose:** Meditation and mindfulness

- **Features:** Guided meditation sessions, sleep aids, stress management techniques, and mindfulness exercises.
- **Why Use It:** It helps users cultivate mindfulness, reduce stress, and improve overall mental well-being.

2. Calm

- **Purpose:** Meditation, sleep, and relaxation
- **Features:** Meditation sessions, sleep stories, breathing exercises, and relaxation techniques.
- **Why Use It:** It offers a variety of tools to enhance mindfulness, promote relaxation, and improve sleep quality.

3. Insight Timer

- **Purpose:** Meditation and mindfulness
- **Features:** Free guided meditations, mindfulness talks, and a meditation timer.
- **Why Use It:** It provides a vast library of resources for both beginners and experienced meditators.

4. Todoist

- **Purpose:** Task management and productivity
- **Features:** Task lists, project organization, goal tracking, and productivity reports.
- **Why Use It:** It helps users stay organized, prioritize tasks, and track progress toward goals.

5. Trello

- **Purpose:** Project management and collaboration
- **Features:** Boards, lists, and cards for organizing tasks, collaborating with teams, and tracking project progress.

- **Why Use It:** It offers a visual and flexible way to manage projects and workflows.

6. MyFitnessPal

- **Purpose:** Nutrition and fitness tracking
- **Features:** Calorie counting, exercise logging, and nutritional insights.
- **Why Use It:** It supports healthy eating habits and fitness goals with comprehensive tracking tools.

7. Grateful: A Gratitude Journal

- **Purpose:** Gratitude journaling
- **Features:** Daily prompts, reflection space, and gratitude tracking.
- **Why Use It:** It helps users cultivate a habit of gratitude, which can enhance overall happiness and well-being.

Recommended Websites

1. LinkedIn Learning

- **Purpose:** Professional development and learning
- **Features:** Online courses, expert-led tutorials, and skill assessments.
- **Why Visit:** It offers a wide range of courses on business, technology, creative skills, and personal development.

2. Coursera

- **Purpose:** Online education and certification
- **Features:** Courses from universities and companies, specializations, and degree programs.
- **Why Visit:** It provides high-quality education on various subjects, accessible to learners worldwide.

3. **Udemy**

- ◦ **Purpose:** Online learning and skill development
- ◦ **Features:** Affordable courses on diverse topics, taught by experts and practitioners.
- ◦ **Why Visit:** It offers flexible and affordable learning options for personal and professional growth.

4. **Reddit (r/GetMotivated, r/DecidingToBeBetter)**

- ◦ **Purpose:** Community support and motivation
- ◦ **Features:** Inspirational posts, personal stories, and advice from a supportive community.
- ◦ **Why Visit:** It provides a platform for sharing and receiving motivation, encouragement, and tips for self-improvement.

5. **Meetup**

- ◦ **Purpose:** Finding and joining local and online groups
- ◦ **Features:** Event listings, group activities, and networking opportunities.
- ◦ **Why Visit:** It helps users connect with like-minded individuals and participate in activities that promote personal growth and social connections.

Positive Affirmations and Quotes

Positive affirmations and inspirational quotes are powerful tools that can significantly influence your mindset and outlook on life. They serve as reminders of your potential, reinforce positive thinking, and help you stay focused on your goals. In this section, we'll delve into the importance of positive affirmations and quotes, how to effectively use them, and provide examples to inspire you.

Importance of Positive Affirmations

Positive affirmations are short, powerful statements that you repeat to yourself regularly. They help reprogram your subconscious mind, fostering a positive and resilient attitude. Here are some key benefits:

1. **Boosts Self-Confidence:** Repeating affirmations helps build self-confidence by reinforcing your belief in your abilities and potential.
2. **Reduces Stress:** Positive affirmations can help reduce stress and anxiety by shifting your focus away from negative thoughts.
3. **Encourages Positive Thinking:** Regularly affirming positive statements helps cultivate a positive mindset, which is crucial for personal and professional growth.
4. **Enhances Motivation:** Affirmations serve as daily reminders of your goals and aspirations, keeping you motivated to achieve them.
5. **Improves Mental Health:** Incorporating positive affirmations into your routine can improve overall mental well-being by promoting a sense of self-worth and positivity.

How to Use Positive Affirmations

1. **Identify Areas for Improvement:** Reflect on areas of your life where you want to see change or improvement. This could be related to career, relationships, health, or personal growth.
2. **Create Personalized Affirmations:** Craft affirmations that resonate with you personally. Ensure they are positive, present-tense, and specific. For example, instead of saying, "I will be successful," say, "I am successful in my career."
3. **Incorporate into Daily Routine:** Make affirmations a part of your daily routine. Repeat them in the morning, throughout the day, and before bed.
4. **Use Visual Reminders:** Write down your affirmations and place them where you can see them regularly, such as on your mirror, desk, or phone.

5. **Believe in Your Affirmations:** For affirmations to be effective, it's important to believe in them. Visualize the positive outcomes as you repeat each affirmation.

Examples of Positive Affirmations

1. **Career and Success:**

   - "I am confident in my abilities and skills."
   - "I am a successful and respected leader."
   - "I attract opportunities for growth and advancement."
   - "I am focused and productive in achieving my goals."

2. **Personal Growth and Development:**

   - "I am constantly learning and growing."
   - "I embrace challenges as opportunities for growth."
   - "I am resilient and can overcome any obstacle."
   - "I am worthy of love and respect."

3. **Health and Well-being:**

   - "I prioritize my health and well-being."
   - "I am strong, healthy, and full of energy."
   - "I nourish my body with healthy choices."
   - "I am calm and at peace with myself."

4. **Relationships:**

   - "I build and maintain positive, supportive relationships."
   - "I communicate effectively and listen actively."
   - "I am surrounded by love and kindness."
   - "I attract positive and inspiring people into my life."

Inspirational Quotes

Inspirational quotes from renowned individuals can also serve as powerful reminders of the wisdom and experiences of others. Here are some impactful quotes to inspire and uplift you:

1. On Positivity:

- "Keep your face always toward the sunshine—and shadows will fall behind you." – Walt Whitman
- "The only limit to our realization of tomorrow is our doubts of today." – Franklin D. Roosevelt

2. On Success:

- "Success is not the key to happiness. Happiness is the key to success. If you love what you are doing, you will be successful." – Albert Schweitzer
- "The road to success and the road to failure are almost exactly the same." – Colin R. Davis

3. On Resilience:

- "The greatest glory in living lies not in never falling, but in rising every time we fall." – Nelson Mandela
- "You may encounter many defeats, but you must not be defeated." – Maya Angelou

4. On Personal Growth:

- "The only way to do great work is to love what you do." – Steve Jobs
- "Your life does not get better by chance; it gets better by change." – Jim Rohn

How to Use Inspirational Quotes

1. **Daily Reminders:** Start your day by reading an inspirational quote to set a positive tone.
2. **Visual Prompts:** Place quotes in visible areas such as your workspace, bathroom mirror, or phone background.
3. **Reflection:** Take a moment to reflect on the meaning of the quote and how it applies to your life.
4. **Sharing:** Share inspiring quotes with friends, family, or colleagues to spread positivity.

Positive affirmations and inspirational quotes are powerful tools for fostering a positive mindset and achieving personal and professional growth. By integrating these practices into your daily routine, you can reinforce positive thinking, build resilience, and stay motivated on your journey toward success. Embrace the power of words, and let them guide you to a fulfilling and purposeful life.

Worksheets and Exercises for Practicing Positivity

Incorporating worksheets and exercises into your routine can help reinforce a positive mindset and ensure the principles of positivity are actively practiced and internalized. These tools provide structured approaches to self-reflection, goal setting, and habit formation. Below are detailed descriptions of various worksheets and exercises designed to help you practice positivity in your daily life.

1. Gratitude Journal

Purpose: To cultivate an attitude of gratitude by regularly reflecting on and recording things you are thankful for.

How to Use:

- **Daily Entries:** Write down three things you are grateful for every day. They can be as simple as a sunny day or as significant as a personal achievement.
- **Weekly Reflection:** At the end of each week, review your entries to remind yourself of the positives in your life.
- **Prompted Entries:** Use specific prompts such as "What made you smile today?" or "What is something you are looking forward to?"

Example Worksheet:

Date	Gratitude 1	Gratitude 2	Gratitude 3
July 1, 2024	A productive work meeting	A delicious lunch	A supportive friend
July 2, 2024	A walk in the park	Learning a new skill	Receiving positive feedback

2. Positive Affirmations Worksheet

Purpose: To develop and reinforce positive affirmations that support a positive mindset and self-belief.

How to Use:

- **Identify Areas of Focus:** Determine the areas of your life where you need more positivity (e.g., career, health, relationships).
- **Craft Affirmations:** Write affirmations for each area. Ensure they are positive, present-tense, and specific.

- **Daily Practice:** Repeat these affirmations daily, ideally in the morning and before bed.

Example Worksheet:

Area of Life	Affirmation
Career	I am successful and valued in my career.
Health	I am strong, healthy, and full of energy.
Relationships	I build and maintain positive, supportive relationships.

3. Goal Setting and Action Plan Worksheet

Purpose: To set clear, achievable goals and outline the steps needed to achieve them.

How to Use:

- **Define Goals:** Write down your short-term and long-term goals.
- **Action Steps:** Break down each goal into specific, actionable steps.
- **Timeline:** Set deadlines for each step to keep yourself accountable.
- **Review:** Regularly review and update your progress.

Example Worksheet:

Goal	Action Steps	Deadline	Progress
Improve fitness	Join a gym, attend 3 times a week, follow a meal plan	July 31, 2024	In progress
Learn a new skill	Enroll in an online course, practice daily, complete project	August 15, 2024	Not started

4. Self-Care Checklist

Purpose: To ensure regular practice of self-care activities that promote mental and physical well-being.

How to Use:

- **Daily Activities:** List daily self-care activities such as meditation, exercise, and adequate sleep.
- **Weekly Activities:** Include activities that can be done weekly, like socializing with friends or pursuing hobbies.
- **Check Off:** Mark off each activity as you complete it to ensure you are taking time for yourself.

Example Worksheet:

Daily Self-Care Activities	Completed (Yes/No)
10 minutes of meditation	Yes
30 minutes of exercise	Yes
8 hours of sleep	No

Weekly Self-Care Activities	Completed (Yes/No)
Meet a friend for coffee	Yes
Spend an hour on a hobby	No
Take a relaxing bath	Yes

5. Positivity Reflection Exercise

Purpose: To reflect on positive experiences and learn from them to enhance future positivity.

How to Use:

- **Daily Reflection:** At the end of each day, write about a positive experience you had. Reflect on why it was positive and how it made you feel.
- **Learning Points:** Note what you learned from the experience and how you can apply it in the future.

Example Worksheet:

Date	Positive Experience	Why It Was Positive	Feelings	Learning Points
July 1, 2024	Received praise from a manager	Felt recognized and valued	Proud, Motivated	Continue to put effort into my work and seek feedback
July 2, 2024	Helped a colleague with a project	Built stronger relationship, felt useful	Happy, Connected	Offer support to others, it's rewarding for both parties

6. Visualization Exercise

Purpose: To use visualization techniques to create a positive mental image of your goals and future success.

How to Use:

- **Find a Quiet Space:** Sit comfortably and close your eyes.
- **Visualize Goals:** Picture yourself achieving your goals in vivid detail. Imagine the steps you took, the obstacles you overcame, and the emotions you felt.
- **Write It Down:** After the exercise, write down what you visualized to reinforce the positive imagery.

Example Worksheet:

Date	Goal Visualized	Detailed Imagery	Emotions Felt
July 1, 2024	Delivering a successful presentation at work	Confidently speaking, audience engaged, receiving applause	Confident, Proud, Excited
July 2, 2024	Completing a challenging project	Working diligently, overcoming challenges, celebrating success	Determined, Satisfied, Elated

These worksheets and exercises are practical tools designed to help you incorporate positivity into your daily life. By regularly practicing gratitude, affirmations, goal setting, self-care, reflection, and visualization, you can build a resilient and positive mindset. Use these tools to enhance your personal growth, well-being, and professional success, and remember that consistency is key to seeing lasting results.

About The Author

Sajeev Kumar K V is an accomplished IT professional with over 25 years of extensive multi-domain experience in both the public and private sectors. Hailing from the culturally rich state of Kerala, India, Sajeev has been deeply influenced by his South Indian heritage and the vibrant tech ecosystem of Bangalore, where he has spent a significant part of his career.

Starting his journey as a Technical Support Engineer, Sajeev's career trajectory has been marked by continuous learning and growth. He has progressed through various pivotal roles such as Network/System Administrator, NOC Lead, Team Leader, IT Infrastructure Manager, and eventually to IT Head. His diverse experience has endowed him with a comprehensive understanding of the technological landscape and the challenges and opportunities it presents.

Sajeev is recognized for his prowess in infrastructure, e-Learning, e-commerce, and cybersecurity. His journey has taken him through various sectors including telecom, construction, manufacturing, and education, providing him with a unique perspective on technological integration across diverse industries. With a Master's degree in Software Engineering (M.Sc), Sajeev is well-versed in IT infrastructure, networking, information security, educational software, Learning Management Systems (LMS), and more.

Beyond his professional achievements, Sajeev is a passionate motivational author. He is committed to inspiring others through his writing, drawing from his rich cultural background and extensive career in technology. His unique perspective as a South Indian techie and motivational author lends authenticity and depth to his insights on maintaining a positive mindset and achieving success.

Sajeev's previous books include:

1. **Digital Etiquette for Youngsters: Being Kind and Safe Online**
2. **Connected Parenting: Navigating the Digital Age with Your Kids**

In addition to his writing, Sajeev's entrepreneurial spirit shines through as the co-founder of a digital marketing and Ed-Tech company. He conceptualized and developed a mock test app and portal tailored for competitive examination aspirants, demonstrating his ability to leverage technology for educational empowerment.

In his book, "Reflections: The Role of Positive Mindset in Achieving Goals," Sajeev combines his technical expertise and motivational spirit to guide readers on how to cultivate positivity and resilience in their personal and professional lives. Through personal anecdotes, real-world examples, and practical strategies, he shares his journey and the lessons learned, aiming to empower others to realize their full potential.

Sajeev's dedication to fostering a positive mindset and his commitment to professional excellence make him a trusted voice in both the tech industry and the realm of motivational writing.

9 798889 519359 4